THE LIFE

AND ADVENTURES

OF AN

ARKANSAW DOCTOR

I was quickly taken off, and found myself in the hands of six big Indians.   PAGE 111

THE LIFE

AND ADVENTURES

OF AN

ARKANSAW DOCTOR

by David Rattlehead

Edited by W. K. McNeil

THE UNIVERSITY OF ARKANSAS PRESS

Fayetteville   London   1989

DESIGNER: Chiquita Babb
TYPEFACE: Linotron 202 Fournier
TYPESETTER: G & S Typesetters, Inc.
PRINTER: Edwards Brothers, Inc.
BINDER: Edwards Brothers, Inc.

The paper used in this publication meets the minimum require-
ments of the American National Standard for Permanence of
Paper for Printed Library Materials Z39.48-1984. ∞

All illustrations are from the 1854 edition of *The Life and Adventures of an Arkansaw Doctor,* Courtesy of Special Collections, the
University of Arkansas Libraries.

LIBRARY OF CONGRESS CATALOGING-IN-PUBLICATION DATA

Rattlehead, David, 1826–1903.
    The life and adventures of an Arkansaw doctor / by David
Rattlehead ; edited by W. K. McNeil.
        p.   cm.
    Reprint. Originally published: Philadelphia : Lipincott,
Grambo, 1851.
        ISBN 1-55728-086-x (alk. paper).—ISBN 1-55728-079-7
(pbk. : alk. paper)
    I. McNeil, W. K.   II. Title.
PS1238.B5L5   1989
813'.3—dc19   89-4692
                                                      CIP

To the memory of James Larkin Pearson,
who, I think, would have enjoyed reading this book.

CONTENTS

INTRODUCTION

THE question arises why one should bother with the writings of a relatively unimportant personality such as David Rattlehead. After all, he was not a major figure in his own time, and the passage of nearly a century since his death has not increased his stature. His biographer doesn't even claim major status for him, referring to him as a minor figure in the history of American humor.[1]

For a folklorist working in Arkansas, there are at least three answers. Published in 1851, *The Life and Adventures of an Arkansaw Doctor* was the first volume solely devoted to Arkansas humor, much of the material being of a folk nature. Furthermore, to echo James R. Masterson, this volume deserves to be rescued from the dust and the mice;[2] filled with a crude and boisterous vigor, it is still readable and enjoyable after more than a century. Finally, it provides a generally correct account of folklife on the Arkansas frontier in the 1850s. Indeed, since there was no one collecting folklore in Arkansas at the time, this book is one of the few accessible sources for Arkansas folklore from the ante-bellum period.

David Rattlehead was the pen name of Marcus Lafayette Byrn, whom his biographer characterized as "a dark star in the mid-century galaxy of Southwestern humorists."[3] He was born at Statesville, Tennessee, southeast of Nashville, on September 4, 1826. His parents, whose names have been lost to history, were apparently comfortable but not wealthy. As Byrn himself put it, "they possessed enough of this world's desirables to give me . . .

a very respectable 'Log-cabin' education."[4] Sometime in the early 1840s, after completing school, he left home on horseback, not to find his fortune but rather to further his education. His employment in a general store ended somewhat disastrously, and he soon was out of that business and on his way to working toward his life's profession.

During his tenure in the store a medical book had come into Byrn's hands. It whetted his interest, and he decided he would devote his energies to becoming a doctor. He began formal studies in the office of a physician near his home and during 1848–1849 was enrolled in the medical department of the University of Louisville. During 1849 and 1850 he spent several months in the Mississippi Valley, taking care of sufferers in an epidemic. In 1850 he attended the Medical School of New York University, receiving the diploma of Doctor of Medicine on March 3, 1851. At some time before 1853 he practiced medicine in Tennessee and Mississippi. By 1853 he moved to New York City, maintaining medical offices there until his death in 1903. In addition to his office practice and correspondence treatments, he busied himself with book publishing, real estate transactions, and, in later years, increasingly with evangelical labors. Byrn took his religion seriously, and his children recall that he never spoke an unkind or profane word.[5] Nevertheless, he was no prude, as *The Life and Adventures of an Arkansaw Doctor* illustrates. A generous man, he was said to be willing at any time to help the needy, either with money or in other ways. In 1898 Byrn went into semi-retirement, moving to a farm near Keansburg, New Jersey, although still keeping a part-time practice in New York City. He spent his leisure time raising cucumbers, watermelons, and blackberries. Early in 1903 he developed pneumonia and died on February 12.

Apparently a gregarious man, Byrn never missed an opportunity to tell stories about his early days in the South, and, of course, he also published them in a series of books that he mod-

estly billed the "most laughable books on earth."[6] Actually, Byrn
passed up few chances to write about a wide variety of topics.
For one who worked full time as a physician, he kept remarkably
busy producing books, all of them in the areas of mail-order
medicine, miscellaneous useful information, evangelism of the
Methodist variety, and popular humor. The first of his medical
volumes appeared in 1852 with the elaborate title *Detection of
Fraud and Protection of Health. A Treatise on the Adulteration of Food
and Drink: with Plain and Simple Directions for Detecting Them; and
of the Deleterious Influence of Lead on the Human System, Means of
Preventing Its Influence, Treatment of Lead Affections, and of the Process
for Detecting Lead Where Present.* This turgid title heads up an extended discussion of the adulteration of flour, coffee, tea, salt,
honey, mustard, lard, beer, brandy, whiskey, candy, starch, and a
few dozen other substances. Byrn was particularly concerned
with the quality of milk sold in New York, much of which, he
says, is from tubercular cows that are kept in cramped and nasty
stables. Two later medical pamphlets were concerned with derma-
tology, and a third one, *The Effect of Tobacco on the Human System
Mentally, Morally, and Physically,* covered much greater territory
while warning readers against the harmful effects of tobacco.[7]
Byrn argues that tobacco not only fills the body with poison and
produces cancer, dyspepsia, and tuberculosis, but it also has
other deleterious effects. These include nervous headaches, out-
bursts of passion, absence of mind, temptation to strong drink,
and suicidal despondency. Byrn further maintains that more than
half of all drunkards, suicides, women of ill repute, lunatics, and
child and wife abusers are users of tobacco. The doctor was
somewhat ahead of his time in advocating a law to ban the sale of
the "filthy weed."

Byrn's other medical booklets included two books on love and
sex in which he insists that love should be treated not as a theme
for pretty poems and wicked novels but as "a great mystery and a
great necessity, lying at the foundation of human existence, mo-

rality, and happiness."[8] He further maintains that it is better to have several disappointments in love early in life than to run the risk of remaining a bachelor. According to Byrn, the best ages for marriage are twenty-two for men and eighteen for women, the woman should always marry a man older than her, and a marriage in which the woman was older could not help but be a troubled one.

Another of Byrn's medical writings, *Solitary Vice. Of the Secret Habits of Youth, Known as Masturbation, Onanism, or Self-Pollution,* also dealt with sex. Among the deplorable results of the "solitary vice" for females was masculinity, bad breath, hoarse or nasal speech, loss of hair and eyebrows, barrenness, frigidity, epileptic fits, and ulcers. That was bad enough, but for the males the consequences were even more dreadful, including effeminacy, nervousness, loss of memory, epilepsy, palsy, brain destruction, and raving insanity; and that was only the beginning. Men who persisted in masturbation could also expect to develop consumption, blindness, rheumatic aches, groin pains, wasting of the backbone, piles, priapism, micturition, stricture, atrophy of the testicles, loss of virility, premature ejaculation, shortness of breath, palpitation of the heart, and spermattorhea, which according to Byrn is perhaps the most frequent result of male masturbation. The doctor says that spermattorhea, or involuntary emissions, at first occur "rarely and in company with a lascivious dream, but later with increasing frequency and at length even in the daytime."[9]

One other of Byrn's medical books deserves mention, especially since it was one of the most frequently reprinted. This is *The Guide to Health; or How to Live a Hundred Years: A Curious and Wonderful Book!,* originally published in 1867 and reprinted in 1870, 1872, and 1876. The promise of the interesting title is not really fulfilled, for this is a miscellany of advice concerning diet, clothing, sleep, the teeth, hearing, chills and fever, bathing, female troubles, exercise, medicines, and various other topics. Byrn suggests that near-sightedness can be cured by rubbing, and thus flattening, the eyeballs.

Byrn's volumes of useful information include such titles as *The Complete Practical Brewer* (1852), *The Complete Practical Distiller* (1853), *The Artist's and Tradesman's Companion* (n.d.), *The Handbook of Science* (1867), *The Farmer's Friend and Home Companion* (1868), *The Magic Mirror* (1869), and *Twenty Ways to Make Money* (1869). All of these booklets contain advertisements of Byrn's other publications, and several contain reprints of his remarks about masturbation. In 1870, under the title *Knowledge in a Nut-Shell*, Byrn published eight of his earlier booklets in a single volume. Two years later, in 1872, he printed *Useful Knowledge or, Repository of Valuable Information*, which included the first 134 pages of *Knowledge in a Nut-Shell*, to which he added 216 pages. This addenda contained treatises titled "Physiology of Marriage and Philosophy of Generation," "Valuable Recipes," and "The Art of Beautifying and Preserving the Hair."

Another subject covered in the doctor's publications was evangelical religion. In 1841, at age fifteen, distraught over the death of two playmates, he was converted at a camp meeting held by the Cumberland Presbyterians near his home town; soon thereafter he joined that church. In *The Singing Evangelist* (1883), a combination songbook and volume of essays on his experiences as an evangelist, Byrn related the circumstances of his dramatic conversion:

Then it was, when hope seemed almost gone and it was my darkest hour in seeking Jesus, I cried out in my agony, "Lord Jesus save me or I perish!"—then came a calm, a quiet, a Holy, a Heavenly peace into my soul—my tears were all dried up, my eyes opened on a new World at midnight on the 26th of that beautiful September night—I knew not at first what to make of it; whether I was on earth or in glory—but at that moment, when those who knew the way, saw that "Christ was in me, the hope of glory"—they shouted for joy at that midnight hour, and

soon I was on my feet shouting the praises of God, the happiest creature in the world.[10]

Byrn's religious enthusiasm was not just a passing thing;
rather it lasted a lifetime. At age seventeen he wrote out his ten
"Rules for Life," which defined his spiritual and moral goals.[11]
But religion was more than just a means of ordering his life; Byrn
also felt it was his duty to preach the Gospel. He started the
Asbury Praying Band and also received a license as "an Exhorter," working in several camp meetings, gospel meetings, re-
vivals, and temperance unions.[12]

Of most interest for present purposes are the Arkansaw Doctor's humorous writings. In addition to *The Life and Adventures*,
these include *Rattlehead's Travels: or, The Recollections of a Backwoodsman* (1852); *Rattlehead's Chronicles* (1852); *Repository of Wit
and Humor* (1853); *The Rambles of Fudge Fumble, or The Love
Scrapes of a Life Time* (1860); *Phudge Phumble's Fillossofy of Phoolishness, a Perpetual Komic Kallender* (1880); and *Vim and Ventures of
Bolivar Hornet* (1886), which was largely plagiarized from George
Wharton's *A Southern Medical Student's Portfolio* (1851). Various of
Byrn's books were reworked and retitled over the years, creating
the impression that he was more prolific than he actually was.
For example, in 1885 he issued *Adventures of a Greenhorn in Gotham!
or, Rawboned Rambles in New York*, which was merely a scissors and
paste rearrangement of *Phudge Phumble's Fillossofy of Phoolishness*
supplied with a totally misleading title.

According to Byrn's advertisements, these books of humor
were "the best selling, most extensively read, and most laughable
books in our country, and at a price within the reach of all."[13] He
also claimed that *Life and Adventures* sold millions, but just how
much faith can be placed in such statements is anyone's guess.
Certainly, some of the humor books sold well, for they went into
several editions, but exact sales figures are no longer available.
That all of his volumes are extremely rare today suggests that the

doctor may have been guilty of exaggerating the sales totals. Whatever the case, the books undoubtedly appealed to an audience sizeable enough to make their further production profitable. Read today, they have a certain period charm, but the humor is very much of its own day. *Phudge Phumble's Fillossofy of Phoolishness* contains 365 entries, one for each day of the year, with several anecdotes or essays after each month's division. For January the reader finds the following sayings:

> 1. Rain or shine to-day if it happens tu be dry.
> 2. Invenshun of Woddin nutmegs in Konnecticut.
> 3. Moon fulls an' emties rapidly.
> 4. Short Wait deskuvered. (It wears wel.)
> 5. Greaze yer boots—if snows kums tha wunt mix.
> 6. Sun Shines—sum whar.[14]

Readers in the 1980s will probably find a typical anecdote entitled "Rather Absent Minded" more annoying than funny:

> I made a mis-hit of it not many evenings ago. I set my four-dollar hat on a hot stove, and did not know but what it was a table until all the best part of it was burnt away and the room full of smoke. I was made, and still I was laughing. I didn't know what to do, so I run out and killed an old maid's cat, split the difference and went to bed.[15]

The jokes and anecdotes in *Rattlehead's Chronicles* are somewhat more comprehensible to modern tastes. One example will sufficiently illustrate the sort of humor contained in the book. On a boat David Rattlehead meets and becomes very friendly with someone he supposes is a lady.

> Well, you think I bit off a piece of her mouth and swallowed it, but I didn't; it wasn't candy, neither; but it was one of the BIGGEST WADS OF TOBACCO that ever was chewed on since Columbus discovered America, that I had sucked out of her mouth, and down it went into my throat and stomach.[16]

By far the most important, and best, of Byrn's several humorous volumes is the very first, *The Life and Adventures of an Arkansaw Doctor*. Although possibly imitative of two earlier popular works of medical humor, Henry Clay Lewis's *Odd Leaves from the Life of a Louisiana Swamp Doctor* (1843), written under the pseudonym of Madison Tensas, and George M. Wharton's *A Southern Medical Student's Portfolio* (1851), Byrn's book is still autobiographical, following his early life fairly closely. Filled with the kind of boisterous horseplay that characterized Southwestern humor, *The Life and Adventures,* its exaggeration notwithstanding, provides a reliable account of cultural life on the Arkansas frontier. Not surprisingly, it is also, albeit unintentionally, a valuable source of early Arkansas folklore. It is particularly useful for anyone interested in traditional medical practices, beliefs of other sorts, folk speech, proverbs, folksong, and, of course, humor.

Considering Byrn's background, it is hardly surprising that he includes much information about traditional medical practices, providing considerable insight into the state of the medical profession in the Old Southwest during the mid-nineteenth century. In one passage Byrn's protagonist has an escapade involving grave-robbing, a common means employed by physicians of that era to obtain human bodies for research.[17] Another misadventure involved the traditional practice of bleeding.[18]

There are, of course, many folk medical practices mentioned throughout the pages of *Life and Adventures*. One character in the book speaks of using asafetida, an anti-spasmodic derived from various plants of the carrot family that is used to ward off colds.[19] A woman tries to cure her husband of an intestinal pain by feeding him a mixture containing large quantities of pokeberry juice.[20] A man with a fever takes a hot brandy toddy to relieve his chills.[21]

Rattlehead is aware that some illnesses are purely psychological, and he resorts to the use of a little psychology in treating these. In these cases he employs folk medical beliefs to bring about his "cure." For example, an old man who believed that a snake had crawled down his throat while he was asleep on a woodpile is tricked by the use of lobelia, a weed that in traditional belief has many curative qualities and is also an emetic. David drowned a small snake in a gourd, blindfolded the old man, and administered the lobelia tea, which worked almost immediately. During one of the old man's greatest upheavals, Rattlehead produced the snake, collecting fifty dollars from the grateful patient, who was convinced he had met the best doctor on earth.[22] As a result, Rattlehead soon gained a good reputation.

A number of folk beliefs that have nothing to do with medicine are scattered throughout *Life and Adventures*. In the grave-robbing episode the traditional fear of touching the dead is commented on.[23] Later, while traveling in eastern Arkansas, Rattlehead tells of watching the actions of his horse to determine the severity of an upcoming storm.[24] There are many folk beliefs that involve observing the actions of horses to predict oncoming weather, and, although the exact version used by Byrn is not found in any folklore collection, it is closely related to many reported traditional beliefs and is probably traditional itself.[25]

Of the folk beliefs found in *Life and Adventures*, none is more widely traveled than the idea that a horse can see a ghost and will balk. This has been reported from oral tradition in North Carolina, Maryland, Kentucky, Alabama, New York, Ohio, and Illinois, and, as Byrn's volume makes clear, was also known in Arkansas.[26] It turns up in an episode in which Rattlehead travels at night through a place that is supposedly haunted. When he gets close to the site "all at once my horse became dreadfully frightened at a ghost, or whatever it was, and would not move a peg."[27] Except for this and the few preceding examples, the folk beliefs found throughout the book play no integral part in the narrative. They are only mentioned in passing and seem to serve little function other than to add a touch of authenticity and local color.

Anyone interested in nineteenth-century folk speech will find

Byrn's account of Rattlehead's adventures a treasure trove. Almost every page contains dialect words. One must be cautious, however, for not everything that appears to come from local dialect does. As were other writers of Southwestern humor, Byrn was inclined to exaggerate or invent words or phrases that looked colorful. Much popular humor of the day, such as that found in minstrel shows, consisted of the distortion of language. Such words as *ramstuginous* owe more to the stereotypes and conventions found in such sources than to folk tradition.[28] But, even discounting the influence of the minstrel show and Southwestern humor, there are many examples of authentic folk speech in the book. Most of these, such as *widow-woman* for *widow*, *diggins* for one's place of residence or employment, and *hain't* for *have not*, are relatively common, but a few items seem to be less frequently reported.[29] One such word is *gubbing*, meaning, apparently, to vomit something; its only known printing is in Byrn's book.[30] The same is true of *Jack's house*, referring to the state penitentiary.[31]

Most of the comments made about folk speech apply equally to proverbs found in *Life and Adventures*. Byrn includes many traditional sayings but also has a penchant for coining new proverbs or rearranging old ones in new ways. Thus one finds commonly encountered phrases like "as still as death," "as white as snow," "Old Harry" (meaning the Devil), and "it always killed or cured."[32] As these examples indicate, proverbial phrases and proverbial comparisons are more numerous here than true proverbs. Several other sayings, such as "certain as three ones make a broomstick," "as plain as an ugly man sees his own beauty," and "like a blind dog in a meat-house," are probably products of Bryn's imagination.[33] They could, however, be sayings he heard that have otherwise been unreported. There can be little doubt that the doctor changed several proverbial phrases for humorous effect; thus he refers to something being "as black as a sheet" instead of the conventional comparison "as white as a sheet."[34]

A few proverbial items make their first printed appearance in

Life and Adventures. This is the case with the phrase "played thunder with" and probably also "drunk as a fool."[35] The latter is also found in Thomas A. Burke's *Polly Peablossom's Wedding and Other Tales,* which also appeared in 1851. It is uncertain which book was issued first; in any case Byrn's usage is at worst its second known printing. Most likely the saying predates the 1850s by several years, for the phrase is cited in Bennett Wood Green's *Word-Book of Virginia Folk-Speech* (1899) as a term of some antiquity.[36] It is also known to have been frequently used by Union soldiers in their letters home.[37] The proverbs and proverbial phrases seem to serve the same basic function in Byrn's book as the dialect items. That is, they are inserted throughout the volume's two-hundred pages to convey a sense of realism and local color. That they also frequently happen to be drawn from oral tradition is just an added bonus for modern researchers; it is also evidence that Byrn relied on something other than his fertile imagination for material.

Lyrics of several folksongs are found in *Life and Adventures,* although only in parody form. Introductory verses in song format accompanied by the title of a suggested air precede each chapter; these pieces are dismissed by James Masterson as being "from mythical sources," by which he means that they are from nonexistent sources. While it is undoubtedly true that the doctor did make these verses up, there is more to it than that. They are a capsule account of what is to be described in the chapter that follows, and they are possibly parodies of then popular songs. Certainly, some of the titles of suggested airs are takeoffs of then current numbers, and perhaps all of them are. For example, chapter 6 is preceded by a lyric said to be sung to the melody "I'll Hang My Nose on a Forked Stick" which is a parody of "I'll Hang My Harp on a Willow Tree," a song still known in folk tradition whose complete history is unknown, but which is frequently said to be of ancient English origin.[38]

Life and Adventures, in common with other volumes of Southwestern humor, contains many jokes and humorous material that seem cruel or crude to genteel readers. A typical example of the pranks from which Byrn attempts to provoke laughter is the account of Rattlehead giving soda and tartaric acid to a drunkard who foamed and spumed for five minutes before he fainted.[39] On another occasion he administers an overdose of croton oil to a young man who pretended to have fallen from his horse but who was really merely drunk.[40] In another instance he breaks up a wedding by releasing hornets under the door of a church.[41] He even witnesses a fight scene, a standard element in Southwestern humor. Generally these consist of much eye-gouging, ear biting, and the like. The altercation viewed by David was between an old man and his wife. When he told her to be quiet she started a regular "buster" that ended with her biting off an inch of his nose. The doctor saved the day by sewing the victim's nose back on with needle and thread.[42]

One of Rattlehead's pranks is a version of a widely known tall tale in which a hog accidentally eats some dynamite and then gets kicked by a mule, causing an explosion that does vast damage and leaves the animal sick for several days.[43] In the incident related by Byrn the animal meets a more tragic end. David feeds a troublesome dog a piece of beefsteak containing gunpowder and a lighted fuse. When the dog exploded "it roared louder than did Bill Saddler blasting rock for beehives on Sunday."[44]

Byrn does not derive humor only from pranks; he also frequently resorts to puns, often of the variety common to the minstrel show stage. Some are obvious, such as when he says, "How do you feel? I don't know how you feel, or would have felt, had you been in my situation, but I felt with my fingers."[45] Others are more subtle, such as this passage in which he toys with the words *scrape,* meaning a fight or some sort of trouble, and *scrapings,* meaning the lowest possible thing in the world: "I had often thought I was in a scrape before, in life, and doubtless you may think I had been, but now I could have got all my scrapes together in a bag, and this would take the rag off your noses; in fact it was the scrapings of creation."[46]

In addition to the elements of folklore already mentioned, *Life and Adventures* also contains references to many aspects of American life that are now mainly a part of the past, such as the bran-dance, corn shuckings, the custom of travelers staying in private homes when they are in a rural region at nightfall, cost marking, and the cold-water pledge of temperance societies. It also contains a wealth of information about cultural attitudes, not only toward ethnic groups but also toward certain tradesmen, such as tin peddlers. Folklore is utilized throughout the volume mainly to provide humor, local color, and a sense of realism. Designed to appeal to a broad public, Dr. Byrn's little book also reflected that audience to a considerable extent. When used with proper caution it reveals a good deal about an Arkansas, and an America, that is gone forever. Undoubtedly Byrn would be amused to know that one of his "most laughable books on earth" is today considered valuable not for its humor but for its depictions of culture on the Arkansas frontier.

W. K. McNeil

PREFACE
TO THE 1851 EDITION

In offering to the public the "Arkansaw Doctor," I make no apologies, nor offer an excuse, more than this: Though I have been born and reared in an obscure part of our country; though my name has never appeared in the public press, and though I have been a roller of pills and masher of boluses in the backwoods,[1] I have as great privileges with pen, ink, and paper, as if I were a descendant of kings and princes. I hope, dear reader, before this work has been scanned by your penetrating eye, that things will have been related that will prove amusing and instructive. I trust you will pardon me for giving a short history of my youthful life; it is not done for self-aggrandizement, but that you may see under what unfavorable circumstances a man may sometimes labor, and yet rise amid every scene of disappointment and blighted expectation, to honor and distinction; and if I should be the means of inspiring one poor desponding soul with confidence, or amuse for a moment some of my fellow beings by relating a few of the many incidents of my past life, I shall be more than repaid for all the labor bestowed on this work.

Raccoon Bayou, Ark.[2]

THE LIFE

AND ADVENTURES

OF AN

ARKANSAW DOCTOR

CHAPTER I

A LUMPING BUSINESS

Air—Gander's retreat from the hog-pen.

When I commenced to rove the world,
*   I was quite young in years,*
And when my banner was unfurled,
*   I melted soon to tears,*
Why I'd left the home of youthful days,
*   My destiny to seek—*
Ah, now how soon the thought betrays,
*   My purse is slim, my frame is weak.*

UNOHO.[1]

HISTORY says I was born in one of the South-western States, in the year eighteen hundred and—bring a bucket of water—in the month of September.[2] What an auspicious moment, or rather, what a lovely month it is. It is in this month we can see the wisdom of nature displayed in all its glory. Think of the rich fruits with which we are blessed, and now, before hoary frost has preyed upon the verdant foliage, all nature seems in its beauty.

But as the month is not so much *concerned now,* with my history, I will leave it and proceed. My parentage I can boast of as being of the highest respectability, but unfortunately, they were not rich—had they been, then this book had never been written. Although they were not wealthy, they possessed enough of this world's desirables to give me and all my other *sisters* a very respectable "Log-cabin" education.[3]

At quite an early age I manifested a disposition to obtain an education superior to that given to my older brothers, or in fact superior to most persons in that part of the country.

I often spoke to my parents about it, and they seemed willing to give me a better opportunity, but they feared my older brothers would make complaint. (Very natural thing in a family, about matters of less importance.) Notwithstanding my desire to obtain an education, I could not help playing many pranks on my schoolmates and teacher, but as these are of everyday occurrence, I will not annoy you by relating them. I went to school about four or five months of the year until I was fifteen years old. I had to work on the farm the balance of the year. Finding at that age that I could not have an opportunity of obtaining much of an education, I proposed to my parents to let me go off about three hundred miles, in a different portion of the state, and offer myself as a clerk in a dry-goods store, with an old acquaintance of theirs. I thought I could find some leisure time to study in an establishment of that kind. As luck would have it, they consented, and now for a long journey thought I. Every preparation for my departure was made. I had as good a horse as ever made a track. The day was fixed for me to leave. I had thought but little about it until the day arrived. What thoughts passed through my aching brain in a few moments. I could think of every endearment that bound me to my youthful home. Yes, even as I recall the scene to-day, after years have passed, it awakens in my bosom feelings of the deepest emotion.

But I must proceed. The day appointed was the 10th of December; it arrived, and I don't think I ever beheld a more lovely day in winter; everything was still as death[4] about that dear old home, that now is lost to sight, perhaps forever. Not the rustling of a leaf, the rippling of water, nothing could be heard save the lonely moan of a dove, perched upon the bough of a neighboring tree, basking in the genial rays of the sun; and well do I remember how desolate and lonely that sound; it seemed as the last dread call to mortal beings on earth. My brothers and sisters were collected at my father's dwelling to bid me a fond adieu; many, many were the words of advice given me before the parting hand was taken; they all took an unusual interest in me as I was going to leave them, to seek my destiny among strangers. Another thing that made them more careful in their admonitions, I was the youngest of the family. One would tell me, "Now, brother, you know you are the runt of the family, any how, and you must be careful—don't get sick—take care of Charley (my horse), and your money." Many other words of advice were given which I have now forgotten—and I s'pose you are glad of it—and I bade them all adieu, mounted my horse and started on my journey. One of my brothers accompanied me a few miles, and then I had to leave him and steer my course alone. Never had I before known what it was to feel bad. I began to wish that I had never started, that I had never left my parental roof. I then thought how kind my parents had been to me. I reflected how I had often treated my brothers and sisters—not but that I had been as good as most brothers, but I thought of the many unkind words I had spoken. I then thought of their attention during any little illness I had ever suffered. I recollected that my dear sisters had come around my couch and wept, because I was sick. I thought of the tears my parents shed when I took the parting hand. I thought of all my schoolmates, how cruel I had treated them, sometimes without a cause—thus thinking, I was overpowered, my youthful heart was filled to overflowing—I burst into tears. This relieved me for a moment, and I knew I had started and it would never do to turn back. I was determined to go ahead. I traveled on until night, and called at a very good-looking house, to see if I could stay all night;[5] I was informed that I could; got down, and after giving many careful directions about Charley, I went in. The landlord was very kind, and made me feel quite at home.

Nothing of interest occurred until I went to bed. I was put into a room with a comfortable wood fire, and being tired from a long ride, I retired early. I suppose I had been in bed an hour and had fallen asleep. I was suddenly awakened by a noise at the door; I was confident the door was locked safe, and that I could not be molested by any person—I spoke, and asked who was there; I received no answer, and hearing no more noise for some time after, concluded I had been mistaken, and was about falling into the arms of Morpheus again when the noise aroused me the second time.[6]

I had prepared myself before leaving my father's to face any difficulty that I might meet, and thought I should soon have an opportunity of trying my weapons of death in my own defense. I accordingly arose, took out my pistol and long knife—the pistol in one hand and the knife in the other—and now I was ready. I still heard the noise at the door. I waited a little while, expecting the door to be forced open—that I should be knocked into a cocked-hat,[7] or eternity, in a little or no time, and then my destiny was soon realized. You had better think I was frequently at my father's house in my imagination, under the same protecting care, but was not long left in my fancied imagination, until the door was opened, and in popped a big black negro almost large enough to swallow me.[8] Says I, "Stop, you black scoundrel, or I will blow your brains out in a moment"—at the same time pointing my pistol at him, and flourishing my long knife in the other hand. I concluded it was a runaway negro trying to rob me. The sight of the knife and pistol had quite a narcotic influence on the

African, for he looked like he had come out of a thunder-cloud in August. He raised his hands to the utmost, rolled his eyes like a Panorama,[9] oped his mouth like the Mammoth Cave, and said,

"Good God! massa, don't hurt poor nigga, him just come to black your boots."

The negro had come to the door, expecting to find my boots outside, and was fumbling about in the dark trying to find them; not finding them outside, he was trying to come in without waking me. I told him to take these and put off, and never attempt to go into a gentleman's room again without knocking, or he might get his spleen blown into a batter-cake.[10] I then locked the door and rested finely all night. On my way next day, I thought about my adventure the previous night, and considered myself fortunate in getting off as well as I did.

In about three days after this I arrived safe at my place of destination, and found my father's old friend. He invited me to see him, which I did very soon, and was not long in telling him my business. A salary was soon agreed upon, and I was getting right up in the world; from a farmer's boy, had become a clerk in a dry-goods store. I felt my greatness, *I did*. I entered on the duties of my calling with a little instruction from my boss occasionally, with due regard for his best interest. The first thing to be done was to learn the whereabouts of all the different articles in the store. This occupied some four or five days, and then my employer said he would give me the pass-word—that is to say, for instance, in particular the cost-mark.[11] I was eager to get into the mysteries of the mercantile business, did not know what I might be some time myself. One morning he came in and said to me—

"Mr. Rattlehead, this is the cost word; you must learn to tell what any piece of goods cost in a moment by this mark, and be careful you don't lose it before learning it."

I took the word and commenced looking over the different goods in the store, and found I could tell very well; but, alas! that word cost me more than it did anybody else. Not being aware of

the vast importance a cost word is to a dry-goods merchant, I
was rather careless with it. The word is one of ten letters, no two
being the same. The word was H-a-r-t-s-f-i-e-l-d. I was going
round looking at one thing and another and their prices, and, not
looking whether any person was in the house or not, I went on
thus: H-one-a-two-r-three, &c., to see if I could tell an article
when it was necessary. A gentleman—or rather I should say fellow, for he was no gentleman that would thus take the advantage
of a boy fifteen years old—happened to be in the store at the
time, sitting down reading a newspaper.

"Ha, ha!" says he, "I've got you now, have I? It spells Hartsfield,
does it?"

If I didn't feel like I was ruined, you may bury me and my
book forever in the oblivion of a potato hill. I told the old fellow
that he was mistaken, it was only the name of a little village
where a friend of mine lived, and I was spelling the name on a
letter I had just written, and was going to send by the first mail.
My lying did not serve as good a purpose in that instance as it did
very often after that with that same old covey, for if I didn't make
him pay for that trick before I got done with dry-goods, then
there is no virtue in high prices. He was a good customer, and he
paid good prices when I was the salesman, certain as three ones
make a broomstick.[12] The old stick-in-the-mud[13] left that day before my boss came in, greatly to my relief. When he came in, I of
course had to tell him all about it, and what a blunder I had made,
and begged that he would excuse me, as I did not know any person was in the store at the time. He looked about as sweet at me
as green persimmons, and pleasing as a rooster laying an egg,
and said nothing for about ten minutes.

Then said he, "We will have to go to work and re-mark every
piece of goods in the house."

I remarked that I was willing to do all that I could. Then we
had it about what word we would have.

Says he, "It is not so easy to find a word to suit every day, and I hope you will be as good to find a word as you were to lose one."

Rather spurred at such a sharp remark, I went to thinking at the rate of a bushel per minute, and in less than a minute I had it. I was always thinking of Charley and my dinner, and here I found the word with ten letters, and no two alike. Says I, "Sir, I've got it for you much quicker than I lost the other."

"Well," he said, "what is it?"

"Charley," says I.

"Charley?"

"Yes, Charley."

Says he, "You are a fool; how does that make ten letters?"

I commenced for him: B-l-a-c-k-H-o-r-s-e, Charley. The thing was so good it put the old boss in quite a good humor, and he and I made *black horse* serve a fine purpose of obtaining high prices for goods after that.

In the store was kept a general assortment of almost every-thing. Hardware, dry-goods, queensware,[14] and a few medicines, &c., &c. After getting over the difficulties about the cost mark, I thought I would get on without any more trouble. Here again I was mistaken. My boss thought he had initiated me sufficiently into the mysteries to trust me for a short time each day in the store alone, while he took his pleasure in walking about. I think it was rather dear pleasure, if I had to guess. He went out one day, and left me in the store. A gentleman called and wanted some blue mass. I went to hunt up the article, and found a jar marked blue mass, and the figures $37\frac{1}{2}$. This I thought was the price of it. I took it down, and sold the jar and contents for thirty-seven and a half cents. I tolled it up, and off he went with near one pound of blue mass for that small price. The price marked on the jar was intended by the ounce.[15]

I was sitting down comfortable, whistling "Yankee doodle," and asked no favors of any man, when in came the old boss. He went to the slate and saw a sale made of blue mass at thirty-seven and a half cents, and went round to see, I suppose, how I had put it up. He looked where the blue mass was, and it wasn't there. He commenced looking at me, and I began to look at him; and says he, "Where's the blue mass jar? I don't see it; have you moved it?"

"Sir, I have sold the blue mass; don't you see it marked on the slate?"

"What! sold all the blue mass in the house for that price?"

"Yes! that was the price marked on the jar."

I have seen bears, wolves, wildcats, &c., staring me right in the face, but he looked more intolerable than anything on record. I remarked to him that I was quite sorry that anything of the kind had happened, but could not help it now, and when he wanted things sold by the ounce he must mark them by the ounce. He considered the matter over, and thought he could not blame me so much, as I was young. I thanked him; and said I hoped nothing of the kind would occur again.

He left me in the store again in a few days, and some person called for tobacco. On the box was marked ten cents. I concluded very readily that it meant by the plug, and told the gentleman ten cents a plug. He said he would take six plugs. I put them up for him, thinking all was right. The ten cents was intended for a square, the plugs being cut into five pieces. The boss came in, and looking on the slate, as usual, he saw the tobacco marked on it, and going round to the box, saw six plugs gone for sixty cents. "Oh, Mol, get off my corns!" what looks. He came near bawling right out; he crammed paper in his mouth, knocked off his hat, and swallowed fish brine. I just thought he'd eat me up without time to say my prayers. He was so mad and so confused he never thought of speaking to me the first time. I took the trouble to interrupt him in his happiness by asking him what was the matter; was he sick or what could make him act so?

"Matter," says he, "you have sold six plugs instead of six squares of tobacco for sixty cents!"

"Well, sir, I know nothing of your squares: I don't believe in masonry, nohow;[16] if you want your tobacco sold by the square yard, just square it off yourself."

Finding that I was a little spunky, he came to his senses again, and we made friends, to my great gratification. He hoped, and I thought, that nothing of the kind certainly would happen again. Believing that I had learned a lesson from the past, he left me again to sell what I could. I was determined on doing better, if possible.

A lady called and wanted some "crockery-ware", among other things a six gallon jar. I went to get it for her in haste, and in my hurry I played thunder with burnt clay.[17] I turned over a pile of vessels that were stacked one upon another, and smashed about five dollars' worth. I thought I had as well be fixing up to leave by the time the old man came in, but then concluding to pacify him a little by selling the jar, I found it, and saw marked thereon twelve and a half cents. It seemed right cheap, but I knew it was none of my business about his prices. The jar (six gallon) went off for the price marked on it. In the evening the old man came in, and saw I had sold a jar for twelve and a half cents. He went round to look for a jar that could be sold for that amount of money. You think you know how he looked, but you don't. There lay the broken jars, jugs, flower-pots, &c., a pile of ruins. He looked at the pieces of hard dirt and then at me; his face looked like a storm rising; his hair raised his hat off his head; his mouth looked as though he was trying to swallow a tea-pot; his eyes streaming with tears; his ears laid as close to his head as a mule's, and there he stood perfectly motionless for fifteen minutes, without being able to say one word. At last he yelled out, "You have broke me!"

"Sir, I beg to differ with you on that point; I have not broke you, but the crockery is knocked crooked, certain. If you and that deformed mud are any kin, perhaps you are broken."

He got madder than ever, and seemed in the act of blowing me up without ceremony, but stopped to ask what sort of a jar I had sold for twelve and a half cents. I told him about the six gallon jar; he could stand it no longer, but made at me as though he intended to give me blazes in a hat-box. I knew I was small, and had better begin in time, so laid hold of the first thing I could get (which was a thunder-mug [18]), and let him have it right in the face and eyes. He stopped about the time this reached him, and commenced wiping off the blood, and thinking. I told him I sold the jar at the marked price. He said that was by the gallon. "Well, what do you measure it in? Unless you leave a big measure I can't sell this sort of stuff by the gallon." He saw the mistake, and said he would look over it one time more. After this we got on without much trouble, and the old man thought I would make a great salesman in a short time. I remained with this gentleman for two years.

Here let me drop a hint or two to young men just commencing business, more especially in a dry-goods store. I thought I must fix myself up considerable after getting a situation like mine. I had one or two suits made at first, and then had to have this thing and that thing, and it all counted by the time my year was up. At the end of the first year I had gone in debt more than my salary considerably. That taught me a lesson that I have never forgotten. The second year my salary was increased twofold, the old boss thinking I would buy as liberally as before. He would caution me about everything else but buying goods from him; he never said once don't be extravagant in your clothing, although he was a professed friend of my parents. The second year I took the precaution of buying but little, and thus hauled out a little of the boss's cash. At the end of the second year I was getting tired of my situation, knowing I could never flourish much in the world as a "counter-hopper," and concluded to resign my office.

During my stay in the store, a medical book chanced to fall into my head—no, my hands. This I read again and again, and cultivated a great taste for the science. How little it takes to make us love those things that are hard to obtain. Many were the castles built by me, in the air, as I thought of studying medicine. I received what was due me from my employer, and started on my return to my father's. I had sold "Charley" during the time I had been in business, as every old hag in the village was running to borrow him, and of course I could not think of refusing, for if I did, they would drive my head into the ground, rock or no rock. In a short time his back was sore, his ribs prominent, tail drooping, and he stood out on the sunny side of the crib looking like he would like to go to the boneyard to get out of his trouble. I went to a landing on the Mississippi River got on board a steamboat, and in a short time was going like the d——l in harness to my place of destination. When I got on the boat I had quite a respectable *little* pile of the "root of all evil."[19] I thought but little of anything, only getting back to my father's to let him see how much I had improved in my appearance, manners, &c. I talked friendly with everybody on board and told them all about my affairs in every way.

Well, trusting to their honesty, I had the consolation of knowing, when I got off the boat, that I had ten dollars left, and was glad I had that much. Big salary for two years' hard labor to show my parents. I felt worse than a blind dog in a meat-house; looked like a drooping turkey-buzzard, didn't know which side I stood on, brought a deep sigh, went into the kitchen, and got as drunk as a fool at a big muster.[20]

My parents thought I had made a decided improvement by going from home, and let me sleep out a long nap that I might enjoy my dissipation to the fullest extent. I awoke, and oh! my head, it felt as lumpy as an old field in dry weather, roared like a saw-mill, and then I *puked.* But enough of this, for most of you know the delightful feeling one has after a dive into Bacchus;[21] so I'll leave you to think how you got over your last drunken frolic, and I'll go on about my own business. I told my parents that I should certainly quit the profession of drunkenness, and take up that of medicine. They thought it would be more profitable and agreeable to me, and equally as desirable to them. I accordingly went to a little village about three miles distant from my father's residence, to see our old family physician, for the purpose of having a talk with him on the subject, and if he said I would make a doctor, it must be so, and would commence immediately. I saw him and he told me many flattering tales, and heads too, about being a professional man, and concluded by saying he believed I would make a doctor if any man in that country would. The terms were agreed on, and I returned home to tell my parents of what had been done. They consented. I was soon ready; and then came the great time that made me an "Arkansaw doctor." The curtain falls. I am sleepy; farewell until to-morrow and then, if I am alive, "my life continues."

CHAPTER II

STARTING OFF
OF THE RIGHT FOOT

Air—The fool's recompense.

The air's composed of certain gases,
That's good when kept together;
But if from that it quickly passes,
It's death on tender leather.

HIM THAT SAW IT

READER, what do you think of our first interview? Doubtless you will say there is room for improvement. I say so too, and I hope, before we reach the other end of nothing, or this book, to amuse you with something more pertinaciously interesting; and now give a turn on the larboard, and off we go, diving into the mysteries of my many mishaps during my studies in the office of my preceptor.

It was in the month of August that I commenced the hottest work of my life, and one that has, as you see already ended in the production of a mass of instruction and amusement for my "feller" men and wimen. The watchword was, never turn back, let the undertaking be good or bad, but go ahead until I had completed my education. I procured me a boarding-house in the little village; and all things being prepared, I went to the office of my intended preceptor. Not finding him in, I thought I must amuse myself in some way, and concluded I could not do so to better advantage than looking over the medicines, books, &c. I laid my hat and gloves on the table and walked around the counter with as much dignity as a young Galen fifty years old.[1] The first thing to be done was to write my name and see how it would look. I commenced, Dr. David Rattlehead. Again and again I wrote it. Then I would write it in co-partnership with some eminent physician; thought what a practice we would have. I thought of being called to see patients just at the verge of the grave, when old and experienced doctors had failed to do them any good, and I would only look at them once, and see the disease as plain as an ugly man sees his own beauty.[2] Then I would give a little medicine, and immediately a change was seen. All the doctors had left me in my glory, and I had cured the case in three or four days. Yes, I thought of being called to see some beautiful and accomplished young lady, the daughter of a wealthy family. She too was fast sinking into the silent tomb; my skills had been heard of, my name heralded through every portion of the country. I was sent for; I detected what had been overlooked by other physicians; the case was put exclusively under my care; I attended her from day to day; I heard her saying, "Doctor, you have saved my life; I never can thank you enough for your kindness and attention." She is restored to health. I visit her and the family often, even when there is no sickness. I talked to her of everything, and love too; I see her blush as I approach: I see she loves me with all the affection of woman: I court her: she leans fondly on my arm and says, "I owe my life to you—my life, my heart, my all is yours:" I clasp her fondly to my bosom: I imprint a sweet kiss on those ruby lips: I have made my fortune: I am completely happy. Hark! I am aroused from my reverie, and see the office full of people:

my pocket-handkerchief is missing: I have swallowed it. I had to give an explanation to the crowd for my strange conduct. I told them that I had embarked in a calling that required the deepest thought, and that I was thinking of the awful responsibility a man took on himself in commencing the study of medicine. I said, "Is it to be wondered that I stood here for half an hour in grand amazement when I have, by coming into this office today, changed my entire course in life, my relationship with the world? I leave today many of my old associates, never again to join in their festivities. I am to-day drinking the wormwood and gall of my life.[3] I bid adieu to the happiness that can again thrill the hearts of my young comrades with pleasant emotions. I shudder as I think to-day closes my hours of happiness and enjoyment with the dear young ladies that have rendered life so desirable; they, with whom I have tasted the sweets of life; they that have poured into my—my—my hat a bowl of soup last week at uncle Bill's quilting. I recollect well enough how Jane Higgs did it, 'cause I kissed Sally Baker. Come in, gentlemen, sit down, you know we all have our faults."

They all took seats, anxious to see how I started, for everybody, and the rest of the world of mankind in that part of the country, said if I "started off of the right foot" I would make a doctor.[4] Well, I was anxious to start off of the right foot too, as you may know. I wanted to make them think I knew a thing or two before reading any thing in medicine, and also wanted to win their good feelings in the beginning, as I had always been told since I had been living, that very much depended on the start we made in anything, and that it must apply to medicine too. I had some good cigars. I got them out and passed them round to all present. As the weather was warm, there was no fire in the office, and I resorted to a match for a light.

My preceptor had prepared a large jar of hydrogen gas for the purpose of making some experiments. In my bustle and hurry, I knocked off the top of the jar in which was contained the hydro-

gen gas, and thereby let in a portion of atmospheric air. To those
unacquainted with this gas, I would say, it is, when mixed with a
certain portion of atmospheric air, a very explosive mixture. I put
the top on the jar again, as I thought, and paid no more attention
to it, not knowing then that any danger was near. I drew a match
briskly across the shelf, and it ignited without any trouble, and so
did something else. If you ever heard a cannon roar on the field
of battle, or shuddered at seven claps of thunder, all in a pile, you
can form some idea of the noise in that office on that day. The
mixture of air and hydrogen had taken fire, and it played the old
Harry[5] with the jar and all the crowd that had collected together
to see me "start off of the right foot." The noise had alarmed the
whole village, and here they came to see what was the cause. In
about one hour, nearly the entire population, including men,
women, and children, negroes, and everything else in the form of
a breathing animal was collected in and around the office. I
scarcely know how to describe the scene. In the midst of the confusion, my preceptor came up and jumped off of his horse in a
rage, and came into the office like fire in stubble,[6] thinking they
were mobbing his student. As soon as he got in he asked me
what was the cause of all this bloodshed, glass, and cigars in his
office during his absence. I related the circumstances as near as I
could. He soon explained the matter to the satisfaction of all
present, except those that had been so unfortunate as to become
the resting place of the pieces of glass. I escaped unhurt, strange
to say, with the exception of a temporary deafness. One man had
his head cut and was bleeding profusely, another his back, another his face, and one poor fellow had a piece of glass drove into
the shank end of his nose. He squealed like a steam-engine,
screamed like a wildcat, roared like a lion, turned over faster than
pumpkins in a thunder-storm, out-spouted a whale, made as
many wry faces as a pig with his tail under the fence, yelled equal
to a greyhound running out of a smokehouse with a ham of meat
in his mouth, and swore he would never go to see a medical stu-

dent "start off of the right foot" again. To tell you the truth, I
thought he made more ado about his wounded proboscis than was
necessary. The crowd could not blame me, as I knew nothing of
what was in the jar, or the danger of lighting a match near it.

This was my introductory letter to my preceptor, and he said
positively, that any man who could come into a physician's office
a perfect stranger to medicine, and in less than one hour blow up
a glass jar, cut right and left on everybody in the house except
himself, and thereby make half a dozen patients for his preceptor,
would make a doctor as certain as four and one make a spit box.[7]
Here ends the second lesson.

Draw my tongue through a watch key, chuckle me under the
chin, take my eyeball for an inkstand, split my lip and poke my
head through it, and come down here everybody that's below,
and up here all ye who are above, and I'll give you my corn-
stealer for a peck basket to feed the pigs out of.

CHAPTER III

SPONTANEOUS EBULLITION
IN A DRUNKARD

Air—Open the gate and let him out.

The drunkard with his thirst unquenched
Came knocking at my door—
"I come to be, and will be drenched
As I have been before."
I told him no; 'twas all in vain,
But soon I did knock under;
Poor man, you will not come again
To see a student's wonder.

FRUNTAS.

AFTER making such an extraordinary start in medicine I felt rather careful, and thought I would use more precaution in future. The next morning being appointed by my preceptor for me to make a formal commencement of studying the healing art, I went according to promise quite early to the office. He was waiting for me, lest I might commit some deed equally as desirable as I had done the day previous. He commenced by telling me the different medicines that were poisonous, and those that I must not touch until I became acquainted with them. He then told me what book to commence reading, and advised me to be a close student and learn as fast as I could. I listened with eager attention to all he said, like it had been law or gospel; told him I would do the best I could, laid off my beaver and went at it.

I had been diving into the hidden mysteries of the science I suppose for an hour or more, when I was interrupted by a sound at the door. I looked up and saw a noted old drunkard, whom I had known for a long time. I knew he was the greatest old pest in the country, and concluded that I was in for a long do-nothing spell, unless I cut his head or his acquaintance at once. He walked in with as much authority as a negro at a corn-shucking and said to me,[1]

"Uh, ah! yes, you look like making a doctor, don't you; I knew you before you was born, and you were no 'count then, nor never will be. Where is the old Doc?"

Says I, "What do you want with him?"

"I want some soda; when I comes in here he gives me some good bilin' stuff."

I told him I knew nothing about his boiling stuff or soda either, and told him to go off and not trouble me, I wanted to read. This only made him worse. I found I had as well try and get rid of him as soon as possible, on any reasonable terms, and got up to see if I could find the soda he was speaking of. I had heard of soda water and seen it used, but knew nothing about preparing it. I was deeply interested in the book I was reading, and wanted to get him off to resume my studies. I commenced looking, and was not long in finding the soda, and near it was the tartaric acid. I put the two jars on the counter, procured two glass tumblers, and soon all things were ready for taking a cooling beverage. Here I was somewhat at a loss to know how to mix them. I did not know which was to be taken first, the soda or the acid; neither did I know how much water or how much soda and acid. I was not to be foiled in my attempts in this way, and thought guesswork was as good as any other when it hit right. I poured each glass about two-thirds full of water. I then put into one glass one table-spoonful of soda, and the same quantity of the acid into the other. I gave him the soda, and told him to drink it. I then gave him the acid.

I had read of explosions by gunpowder, and bursting up of steamboats, railroad accidents, and hailstorms; but that laid every-thing in the shade,[2] and Bill Measles besides. The old fellow made for the door, put one hand on each side, threw his mouth open, stretched out his neck about a foot, shut his eyes, and then, if ever you saw water boil, it boiled out of him in a stream as big as your arm. For near five minutes his mouth was a living fountain. I thought the man would certainly burst open. His stomach roared like distant thunder; his eyes, starting from their sockets, looked like the full moon rising in midsummer, and his nostrils, distended to the size of a dog's mouth, looked like one side of creation. In his pouting he threw off more bread than would kill an Irishman, more beef than would fatten a dead negro, more oysters than would choke a turkey-gobbler, more mackerel than would make a nice supper at a boarding-house, and more gas than would make lies enough for a political demagogue in two speeches. He continued his upturning of gastric forbearance for about five minutes without being able to open the door of his respiratory prolongation. I saw him begin to turn as black as a sheet;[3] his frame trembled, his hands lost their hold, and down he came like a log of wood in winter at the door of the office.

> Fire and water,
> Mud and mortar,
> Beef and hogs! what a slaughter.
> Old man, may I have your daughter?[4]

What a scrape I am in again; the most unfortunate man in the world; never went to do anythings in my life but I was making some mistake; but I'm in for it again, and must get out the best way I can. Here came the whole village again, bellowing like so many calves in a farmyard. In less than fifteen minutes I had a crowd at the office large enough to storm a fort, and fools sufficient to kill any man with as much sense as would go round your hat. One smart old gentleman wanted to know what I had done to the man. I told him of the old drunkard wanting soda, and that I had given him some to get him to go off.

"*Pisen'd! pisen'd!*" was the cry raised instanter, and off some one went to find my preceptor, or some other physician, that could tell what to do. In the excitement some person mistook *pisen'd* for *fire,* and then the tune was changed to *fire! fire!* Everybody broke like doctors from a graveyard, as they knew I always kept a little "powder" about, that was hard to put out when once it took fire. Out they ran, and in a little less time than a merchant can tell the truth, we had a deluge of water pouring into the office.[5] Such a rattling of buckets, washbowls, slop tubs, and salt barrels, has not been heard since Job killed the "fat turkey."[6]

I have often heard persons blamed for raising a false alarm of fire, but this was one time it did good. The poor old drunkard lying there in a state of suspended animation from his long spouting spell, was aroused by the cold water. He bawled out, and wanted to know if the "second floor" was coming: being informed by many voices "no," he raised himself up about six feet high, sprung out of the door like a blue streak of lightning or "Moffat's pills" was after him,[7] and ran home to his wife, promised her never again to trouble a medical student, signed the pledge, and has never been known to touch a drop of the "critter" since.[8]

CHAPTER IV

THE RESURRECTION, OR HOW TO TAKE UP A NEGRO

Tune—You dig and I'll watch.

If doctors go to seek a prize
  Among their patients dead,
They must be bold, they must be wise
  To save them from an aching head;
And if when they have once began
  To dig and raise the sod,
They must not stop, though dog and man
  Should come all in a squad.

GOURDHEAD.

AFTER the trouble with the drunkard, things went as well as I could expect for several days, considering that I was never known to be out of some sort of scrape for more than a few days at a time. As I was the first student the old doctor had been troubled with for some time, he was out of a skeleton. This desideratum had to be met as soon as circumstances would *assist*. We were not long left in want of an opportunity to obtain one. My preceptor had a patient, a negro, that had been sick for some time with a chronic disease, and who was destined to fall a prey to its influence very soon. The patient died, and amid the heartfelt sorrow of the owner for his loss, and the numerous explanations of the old doctor why the disease had terminated fatally in spite of all remedial agents, he was interred in the silent grave with as little ceremony as is usual on such occasions. My preceptor returned home after staying with the patient until his *last expiring moment,* and told me that as I had just commenced the study of medicine, and would have many trying scenes to pass through before I made a doctor of myself—he wanted to see whether I would do to "tie to" or not,[1] and said, that on the next night I must be ready to go with him to take up the negro that had died the night previous.[2] I told him I was in, and he might depend on me as being as good as ever fluttered, and said to him, "If I grunt, make an ugly face, or turn up my smeller for the first time you may kick me out of the office to-morrow morning, and drive me twenty feet in an ash pile, never again to rise until old 'Pidey's' horn grows off."[3]

He remarked very calmly that as for him he was an old hand at the business, and never thought of being armed about trifles, any more than a Yankee does of selling goods under first cost, or a tin peddler of passing a farm without his share of the gatherings of the longneck squallers.[4]

There was one part of the "undertaking" that rather puzzled us: the old doctor and I were both small, and not able to do much more hard work than a dozen Irishmen,[5] and therefore would need some assistance. He would have to employ a man, and the difficulty was of getting a man that would not become alarmed when we most needed his assistance.

My preceptor, like every doctor, had many debts owing him by the poorer class, that he knew could never pay him and thought that would be the best chance to get a man to assist. He put off in the "hollows" to see a man that was owing him a bill of some size, and finding him in the woods mauling rails, all in a crowd by himself,[6] he told him if he would go and help us, he would credit his account for five dollars. The fellow was glad of a chance to pay up, and agreed to be with us on occasion. The hour and the place were named for us to meet.

My preceptor told me of the arrangement, and said we must not go off together, or something might grow out of it of a serious nature; and told me at the same time of the dreadful responsibility, and that should we be caught and the law enforced, we would both go to "Jack's house" for the term of three years.[7]

This news played thunder with my bravery.[8] I felt like I was fifty feet in the air and nothing to hold to; thought how the doctor and myself would employ our time in the State prison; would they let him follow his profession and practice among the convicts, and would I roll pills for him as usual? How sorry my old mother would feel—and worse than all, I could not get to see my angel sweetheart any more, for she would never have me after I had been in prison. Oh! horrid thought—why did I ever commence such a profession? why was it I had not thought of these things before commencing? what was I to do? do like they do over the river? do without saying any more, or thinking of it in any way? I eventually reconciled myself to go through it at all hazards. The night appointed arrived; eleven o'clock, and everything was still as death in that little village.[9] I waited the moment; I turned the key of the office and started. Going round a little string of fence at a certain post, I might have been seen, if it was daylight, but it wasn't, moping my way in the dark, hunting for a spade and an old bag. The bag was intended to put the negro in. I found them, went and saddled my horse, mounted, and soon was on my mission of grave-robbing for the first time. I went on until I arrived at the place appointed for us to meet. I then whistled, and was answered by my preceptor and his assistant. It was in a dark skirt of woods, where we could not distinguish a man from a hornet's nest, only by the "feel."[10] We met, and then for the grave-yard; it was near the woods. In a short time we reached it;

and it was then a time to talk about gravery over a dead negro. We all went walking as easy as a cat on straw, round and round the grave.[11] I kept waiting to hear what the old doctor was going to say. I waited for some time in the greatest agony, and not a word was spoken. His bravery he had showed more before reaching the field of glory, and he had forgotten to bring it in his saddle-bags, and there he was without any. Getting tired of waiting, and finding I was more composed than he was, I said to him, "Doctor."

"Don't call my name, you fool you."

"Well doctor," said I, "if you have come here to get up the negro, let us be at it right off."

"Well," said the doctor, "you and Dick work awhile and I will watch."

I told him to go a piece from us and listen for the approach of danger; that he must be very alarmed about taking up an old negro, and him dead as a forty year old trout.[12]

I tried to appear very bold to the old doctor, but I can tell you I felt a little of the awfulest I ever had, up to that time, and had it not been I thought my preceptor was trying to scare me, I would have felt worse than a sheep in the forest at midnight.[13] He went off a piece from us, and Dick and I commenced operations in earnest; he digging, and me giving directions and feeding him occasionally on old whiskey to keep up his strength and spirits. We were working away at a great rate when we were interrupted by the sudden approach of my preceptor, puffing and blowing worse than a steamboat in a fog on the Mississippi.[14] He came up, and said that they were after us. Dick dropped the spade as quick as though it was hot; I dropped the bottle of whisky as slick as if it were an oyster or the white of an egg, and off we all went, faster than a rabbit with forty dogs after him in an old field. We went until we reached the thick woods, and there stopped to await the result. Very soon we found it was a false alarm.

I rebuked the old doctor sharply for his chicken-heartedness,[15] notwithstanding I felt myself as though I was not larger than a pound of soap after a hard day's washing. I told him he need not watch for us any more, as he would do more harm than good. My *apparent* boldness gave him a little self confidence, and he concluded he would stay with Dick and me the rest of the time. We commenced again, and were getting on as well as a sinner at a camp-meeting, not fearing anything or anybody. The night was fast wasting away, and we had much to do before the approach of bright morning. As our "deeds were evil," we sought darkness rather than light, and must finish before daylight. We worked rapidly and gave little attention to surrounding objects. We had nearly secured our prize, and the doctor was getting brave again. Dick was doing his cleanest, best, and—bim—

"Halloo! what is the matter, Dick?"

"I have got to the coffin," says he.

Here we were in a nice fix; we had come off from home without anything with which we could open the coffin. The doctor became very much enraged at his own negligence, talked really *loud* and plain, and said he would not be disappointed in any such way. There was a rail fence about one hundred yards from where we were. He went to that and got a big rail and brought it to the grave.

"Let me get there a moment, Dick."

He took the rail, turned one end down, and in a short time he had the top of the coffin knocked in, sure enough. Then came the trial, who would go down and lay hands on the *subject*.[16] The doctor said he thought he had done his part, and proposed to Dick to go down. Dick did not say much, but grunted worse than a man with the toothache going for a load of wood,[17] turned up his nose a little like he smelt something, and thought he had worked harder than either of us. I began to get tired of hearing so much talk about a small matter, threw off my coat and went down. I was in the act of fastening, a rope round the negro's neck, by which he could be pulled out, and was congratulating myself that

I should have the praise next day for my daring and fearless conduct. I fancied the skeleton hanging up in my own office; I thought of the pleasant times the doctor and I would have in the big cave we were going to take him to; I considered the danger all over, thinking everbody was asleep at that late hour; and now for a—hush! hush! what has happened? I heard a noise in the upper world like the heaving up of a volcano. I heard the dogs barking, chickens flying from their roosts, geese running and flapping their wings equal to knocking the two ends of creation together; the cows lowing, and the sound was like the last sad sound of the hunter's horn; bushes cracking, sheep bleating, and, to cap the climax, an old owl as big as a whisky barrel, hollowing loud enough to raise tadpoles out of water. I had not time to think what was the matter before I heard my preceptor cry out, "Good God!" and away he went as fast as legs would carry him. Dick bawled louder than a two year old calf turned loose in a hailstorm, and that was the last of him too, for he was so scared that he would not have known an ox-cart from an elephant. Well, if ever I was in a real "quandary" I was then: there I was, left in the grave with none to keep me company but the dead negro, and not so much as a stick to assist me out of the grave, which was very deep. I thought I was doing my last job on earth, or rather *in* the earth, and that not a very desirable one, considering the consequences.

I was not long in thinking what to do. I knew if any persons were after us, that unless I got out of that place my time was up. I squatted down like a dog going to jump a fence, made one powerful exertion, and out I came slick as butter out of a hot skillet.[18] I took to my heels as hard as I could go, not looking to see what the noise and confusion was all about. Dick and the doctor were not far ahead of me, and I soon got up with them. We all run for life, not stopping even to see what sort of rails were on the fence, but, jumping over, or trying to, we knocked down about two hundred panels of it, making as much noise as an earthquake. The noise of the fence falling alarmed our horses, which were tied out in the woods nearby, and they commenced pulling harder than a woman that wears the breeches hold of her dear husband's nose. Their pulling, like the candy-maker's, was not in vain, and soon they broke loose, and away they went like buffaloes from a prairie on fire.

Of all the fixes that *Tom Knowling* and *Bill Chumny* ever got into since *Blithersdorf* had the neuralgia,[19] we were in it then. Our horses were gone; the grave open, a hole knocked in the top of the coffin; my coat, Dick's hat, and the doctor's old saddle-bags, being close around. I thought—and then I thought I had not time to think any thing about it—and about the time I got to thinking, I thought the dogs were after us, and they were. We had got off some few hundred yards from the grave-yard when I heard the loudest, the longest, the keenest yelling of greyhounds, little fierce bob-tail curs, and bull-pups, that ever screamed this side of the Rocky Mountains. On they came, making more noise than a thousand old women at a quilting, after us. I felt most awful, but could not help laughing at Dick and the doctor. They kept trying to swallow each other to get out of the way of our pursuers, and had it not been that they commenced at the wrong end, they would have accomplished it. While they were at this, the dogs kept coming with all the speed of their feet, heads and tails.

I saw something had to be done about as quick and as slick as swallowing an oyster, and told them to hold their horns a moment and I would tell them how to do. I went a few steps and found a bending tree that I thought we could climb. I heard a loud shrill halloo in the distance, and the dogs commenced worse than ever. I just expected they would have us all for breakfast next morning. (Thought if they did, they would have as tough pulling at Dick's carcass as medical students on bull-beef at a boarding house at three dollars a week.) I spoke to my two companions and told them of the bending tree; they were as glad to hear it as a negro is at the sound of the dinner horn in cotton picking time, and came to me as soon as I named it. We all hur-ried up the tree, and had barely time enough to get comfortably located before the dogs came up and said good night to us, stopped, and seated themselves at the root of the tree. We looked down on them with contempt, until we thought probably their backers were not far off. I thought of a great many things in a short time; among other things, thought what a fool I was that I did not get sick before leaving home and stay there. This think-ing then, did about as much good as rubbing your nose with a cow's horn.[20]

Very soon we discovered the source from which this human bellowing proceeded, as we could distinctly hear persons talking and encouraging the dogs. I had often heard of persons being tree'd, but this was the first time I ever saw people in good ear-nest "tree'd." Well, how could the persons at the house tell we were all at the grave-yard taking up the negro? Somebody be-trayed us; can't help it now: we'll be shot out of here when daylight comes.

The owners of the dogs came up (the owners of the dead negro they were), and looked all round to see what tree the dogs were at. The dogs commenced barking at the root of the tree we were in. There was another tree standing two or three feet from the one we were in. After looking a few moments, I heard one of the men say,

"Boys, we'll cut it down."

My old straw hat and Jack Cooper![21] how I felt when I heard that. I could not have felt worse on a bar of iron in the Atlantic Ocean. I now saw and soon would feel what it was to learn to be a doctor. They commenced cutting, the tree was small and it must soon fall, and then we will—will—all get knocked into eternity. What now was to be done? If we hallooed it would only make it worse; they would kill us anyhow: we must all die when the tree falls. I heard Dick making his last compliments to his Maker. He said:—

"My old providence in heaven and earth, I am come to it now; have mercy on me, for you know I stole Gills' meat, and he starved. I won't do so no more if I die. Take care of Polly and the children, and don't let them work old Paddy in the slide agin. And oh! how sorry I am I didn't stay at home, and—and—fare-well—oh! here I go—oh!"

And down came the tree, but it was the one standing near to us. As the tree struck the ground they set up an unmerciful yell-ing, dogs, men, and all together—and what do you think it was about? it was an old fool coon that happened to be in the tree resting himself. The dogs bounced on him like a duck on a June-bug, and used him up in a short while.[22] The men boasted of their dogs for a short time, how they went out at night without any-body with them, and tree'd a big old coon worth two bits in old whisky the next "muster" they had in town, and put off home. How good we all felt. After they got out of hearing, Dick let off his breath like he hadn't breathed for two hours, and said he felt very thankful to me for naming to them of the tree. We all slid off that tree like terrapins of a hot day, and it was only two hours to-day. I told them, when we commenced anything we must go through it. We went back to our work, and without much more trouble we got up the negro and carried him to a cave, a short distance off in the side of a hill, covered him up safe, and started home to see what had become of our horses. We found them safe at home, and by the time we got all things to rights it was day. My preceptor never boasted any more about his spunk. Dick said he wouldn't be a doctor for the world, and I said but little, know-ing I had rather slashed the old doctor on the first heat.

Hold on—hand me a fly with a little wanillifidity on it; hush your gab and take that worm out of your mouth! Here we will go to dinner.

CHAPTER V

BUSTING A DOG
AND CARVING A TURKEY

Air—Puley died with the hollow horn.

Dogs are useful animals
*   If they are kept at home,*
But worse than any cannibals
*   When in doctor's shop they roam;*
And turkeys are the finest dish
*   While they are young and tender—*
But if they're tough, I never wish
*   Myself to act as carver.*

SHITEPOKE.[1]

WELL, now I have recovered from negro-stealing and loss of sleep, and will endeavor to give you a little more of my experience in life. After attending the big cave every night for two weeks (where I had been dissecting the negro), I again commenced studying regularly. I was not long left at ease, and in a situation to enjoy my reading. A strange circumstance took place at the office; I began to think I was haunted; I felt extremely uncomfortable. There was a large dog in the village belonging to a gentleman of the highest respectability. I am constrained to say this from the fact that I loved his daughter about as hard as a mule could kick in a "yellow-jacket's" nest.[2] I was a frequent visitor at his house, and the family seemed to think me quite deserving, for they never said anything about me but in terms of highest praise. I had often noticed the dog, but did not see that there was anything peculiar about him. When I first commenced visiting the family, the dog tried, on several occasions, to "insert a tooth" for me, but my visits becoming more and more frequent, he found it troublesome, gave it up as a bad job, and became very familiar with me. I had been visiting the family, or rather Miss Mollie, for I cared but little for any of them but her, for some time. From some cause, I can't tell what, the dog commenced returning my calls, and he came to see me as regular as the sun rises. I began to feel rather bored with such a customer; not that I entertained any unpleasant feelings toward the dog, but it was something so unusual, so much out of the ordinary habits of the animal. He would not go to any other place from home, and would not come to the office only at that particular time, which was just after sunset. I was getting on the superstitious order, though I was no believer in "ghosts."[3] Every little boy in the place was annoying me about being so intimate with Colonel Tilford's family. "Even," said they, "old Cuff comes to the office every day to see you." Then the old women got hold of it, and it had as well been in the papers: and, to make it still more desirable, the negroes got to putting their clap-boards of locomotion in use on the subject. I was mad, I was sad, I was teased, I was greased, and squeezed about the affair until I got as mad as Davy Crockett and the bear in the hollow tree.[4] I knew as well as I was a rogue that it would not do for me to make any public demonstration of my displeasure, for that would only make things worse. I was careful not to let anyone know that I felt a little "haunted,"[5] as that would, perhaps, lead to suspicion that I had

been doing something wrong. I therefore determined to get rid of
the dog, whether it was ghost or no ghost; for unless I did, my
studies would be knocked into a candlestick without wick or
tallow.[6] You need not be thinking any such thing; I didn't intend
to poison him: I was too high minded for that.

I concluded, as a first resort, to give the dog a good thrashing,
and thought, perhaps, that would give him the hint that his company was not desirable. I procured me a long beech limb, large
enough to drive oxen with, and had it ready by the time he would
come the next evening.

As faithful as ever, about halfway between sunset and dark,
while everybody was at supper, and the others doing something
else, here he came, walked into the office with as much authority
as a big bob-tail rooster into a hen house,[7] and commenced going
round and snuffing like he smelt something. I said to him—

"My old fellow, I'll give you particular thunder one time, and
then, perhaps, you will stay out of here; I'll not have everybody
talking about you running after me like we were some kin."

I took the precaution to close doors on him, got my beech limb
and commenced on him. "Well, please to clear the dishes off,
will you?"

If ever a man was deceived in this life, I was that time. The old
dog, instead of rearing and charging like a little ram at a gate-
post, to get out, told me in language that could not be misun-
derstood, that it was a two-handed game. He gave me one hoarse
growl, and made at me like a tiger. I saw I was in for a bad *scrape;*
turned round as quick as I could, thinking if I would open the
door he would go out and say nothing more about it. As I turned
he made a grab at me, and caught me about six inches below the
middle of the back. He jerked me down as slick as you could
swallow castor oil before breakfast. He commenced on me in re-
ality, and I thought that I was to die one of the most undesirable
deaths that ever came along. He held on to his hold and shook
my two extremities together as easy as if I had been a snake. I

thought of hollowing,[8] but then I knew that would not do, the beater beat. I finally concluded to send him a flag of truce: I did so by saying to him, "Cuff, Cuff," and whistling to him. It had the desired effect; he dropped me like a hot potato,[9] to see who was calling him, and I opened the door that he might cool down a little. He went out after staying as long as he wanted to.

Now wasn't I mad? I thought of every means to retaliate; I walked in every direction, knocked my head against the wall, threw off my coat, rolled up my sleeves, and then, in the absence of something better to do or do with, I fell down, rolled over faster than an old log in high water, and bleated equal to billy-goat at a cornpile.[10] I found such snorting and prancing would never kill the dog, and as I was determined on his life, I cooled and commenced thinking. I could not stomach the thought of poisoning him, it looked so much like negro revenge.[11] What was I to do? I knew it would not pay well to shoot him; I was unwilling to try my knife on him, lest he should apply the scarificator to my *sternum* again. There I stood, looking kin to a fool at a brandance;[12] but you know I soon start something important when I get to thinking right hard. My thoughts had availed me much in equally as tight places, and I was certain they would come to my rescue now. In a little less than no time I "had it." Ah! revenge, 'tis sweet I'll show you, my old dog, how to growl.

I was certain that dogs would eat meat when they could get it. I resolved on trying another experiment, to see who would come off conqueror. I procured some pieces of raw beef, spunk, and half a pound of gunpowder. About the time I thought he would pay his evening visit, I got all my things ready. The pieces of beef had been selected for the purpose, and they were in hunks as big as a miser's heart.[13] I had five or six of those pieces. I cut into the beef and hollowed it out, each piece, so that it would hold near an ounce of powder. After having them all charged with powder, I got the spunk[14] and prepared a piece of it for each of the beef, by cutting into the middle, touching it with a small piece of fire, and then sealing it with a wafer. This being put with the powder, and a string tied fast round the beef, I threw them to the dog, and, as I had expected, he swallowed them without chewing. I soon had five ounces of powder "safely" lodged in his gastric cavity, and he wagged his tail for more, like he thought I was a great friend of his. I told him he couldn't come it, and ordered him out.[15] He did not seem disposed to go, and I began to fear the fire and powder would grow warm in their digestive movements. I had rather been caught stealing watermelons, than for the powder to have taken fire while the dog was in the office.

When driven to it we can do many things, and I knew one of us had to be out of there pretty soon, or I would be in as bad a fix as the dog. I started out in as great a hurry as a man with diarrhea. As I went out I saw a bucket of water, and in a moment I recollected that dogs were as fond of water as doctors of poor patients. I took up the bucket and threw the contents on the dog. He shot like an arrow out of the back door, and then as I must see the fun out, I shut up the doors and started to supper.

I think it was the best time for a little amusement of this kind that ever happened. The inhabitants of the little village were all standing on the sidewalk talking very busily just after sunset, on a beautiful day in fall. As I got out the front door I saw the dog some few steps from me, trotting along as big as an Irishman with a jug of whisky on Saint Patrick's day.[16] He went a few steps further and belched forth. It was rich! *it was*. I never have witnessed anything more interesting for the same length of time. It roared louder than did Bill Saddler blasting rock for bee-hives on Sunday. Such another noise had not been heard in that place since everybody collected together to see me "start off of the right foot." The whole village was soon on the spot, except myself. I thought that I had better stay away for a while, to avoid any suspicions resting on me about killing the old man's dog. I went in and got my supper and could stand it no longer, but put off to see "What was the matter." I went up, and there was a sight for a man that had recently taken his supper. The good people were standing about in perfect amazement, none daring to go nearer than ten or fifteen feet of the remains of the dog. The animal had been torn asunder, and no mistake, and his quarters were thrown in as many different directions as a Yankee has ways to make a living.[17] Next evening the dog came to see me, *he didn't.* Then came the tug! who did it? Well, there was no proof; but there was no one in the village that had aught against the dog but me, and I therefore had to labor under the suspicion of killing old "Cuff."

Now for another scrape! I had not thought of the importance of the affair. I was awfully in love with the old man's daughter, as I said before. I expected nothing else but a blow up of my expected happiness. Ah! yes, I was soon to be driven from that angel's presence, that I had loved as my own soul; no more was I to bask in her sweet smiles; no more to kiss those precious lips. We were plighted to marry at the end of my studies. (Two years.) We could afford to wait that long, as we were both young. But now farewell to every hope of such happiness; it was gone forever. I resolved on seeing her at all hazards, one time more. I did not wait long, fearing the excitement would get "no better fast." The next evening I went as usual to see Miss Mollie. I expected to get my walking papers[18] about killing old "Cuff;" the whole family thought he was a great dog. I went in, and immediately I saw a change; they all looked as sweet as rye biscuit at me;[19] Miss Mollie did look a little more natural than any of them, but even she did not look right straight at me. The first thing to be talked about was the departed dog. I made very strange of it, and said any man who would be guilty of such a thing was a low-bred, mean scoundrel. I saw it wouldn't take and as soon as possible changed the subject to one more agreeable. I never experienced such feelings in all my life. To think of being ruined about blowing up a dog, was intolerable. I tried to talk; my mouth wouldn't go off. I saw at once I was only treated with the civility that I was, for some sinister motive. I made a rather short stay of it, and on my departure was greatly surprised to receive an invitation to a "little gathering" they were going to have next evening. I felt a little easier after this, but still feared something was going to be done to me. I could almost always tell when a storm was rising over my head, by my feelings. I thought I would go, and if anything went wrong I would be in for another buster. My dander was up as big as an elephant, and, reader, I will make you think so before I am done, mind if I don't.[20]

Well, the time appointed drove round and told me to get in: I did so, and found a dozen or two of the best looking young folks in our place, seated round, talking and laughing like something was to come off soon, and thinks I, it is all to be at my expense, and then won't it be awful before such a crowd to be exposed and lose dear Mollie too. I didn't feel much like talking under such liabilities, but I was thinking about as hard as ever you saw a man in all creation.[21] While I was thinking at such a rate, the old lady and gentleman came in, and explained the object of the meeting by asking us in to supper. We all walked in, and I saw what they were "up to." The old lady politely requested that I would "cut up" the turkey. I told her I was a poor hand, but was willing to do the best I could. I had never carved a turkey in my life, and knew about as much of the science as I did of the French language, but saw there was no getting out of it, and pitched at the old fellow like lawyers at a large estate.

Oh, will you just kick me off my moral subsistinance: Of all the turkies that ever yelped on chestnut ridges, this beat them. It must have been the gobbler that Noah turned loose. And then the knife—it was dull enough to go to mill on.[22] There I was, doing nothing as fast as you could drink whisky, and everybody waiting to try their teeth on the "herbiferous." I had hold of his hind leg above the knee with one hand, and the knife in the other. I found that I had as well try to drink the Mississippi dry as to cut that tough old gobbler. I was getting red in the face; I was panting for breath; the whole crowd laughing at me; I began to throw aside modesty and take up a little of something more profitable; bravery. I was as mad as a Jew when he gets the price for an article that he first asked.[23] I would die rather than be beat. I cooled down a little. I held on to my hold as I quietly commenced pulling the old trotter off of the dish—still I sawed away—I got him on the table—I kept sawing until I got him on the floor—here I did not stop either—I hauled him to the door—made him give one good "cute," with my assistance—and then taking my foot instead of my hand I kicked him twenty-feet into the yard.

"Madam, will you please to kill your turkey before bringing him on the table, when you ask me to combat one again?" Great was the consternation when the old gobbler made his exit. The old gentleman raised up, and made at me with the vengeance of a maniac. I did not want to hurt him, and concluded the best policy would be to leave while my credit was up. I broke for my hat, which was on the other side of the table—I grabbed it, and at the same time started out at the back door. As I stooped to get my hat, one of my coat buttons caught in a hole in the table-cloth, and off came the old lady's "China," with the crash of a falling temple. The old man, forgetting himself for a moment, called old "Cuff" to catch me; but I had no fears of "Cuff" then, he had gone where all the "good dogs" go. It is unnecessary to say that this broke up my love scrape with a rush.

> "Yonder sits a wild goose on that tree,
> I look at him and he look at me;
> I cocked my gun, he saw me raise it,
> He owes me a debt, I know he'll not pay it."[24]

But never mind, old "Rackensack" is never behind only when he aint before.[25]

Three sticks of cough candy, one wooden nutmeg and a cow's heel—Farewell! May you never know one sorrow, may your life be one of uninterrupted happiness, and may your heart never throb but with feelings of tender emotion. The cloud is lowering over me; I'll tell you about it to-morrow.

CHAPTER VI

THE WAY TO KEEP
FOLKS FROM MARRYING

Air—I'll Hang My Nose on a Forked Stick.[1]

How sweet to love when loved again;
How bad it is to suffer pain;
How happy are we to win a heart;
How bad it is with it to part.
How bright the night on which they met;
How soon they found a room to let;
How rich would been the bridal ring;
How they would envy prince and king.

SHAKESRAG.[2]

I DID not call on Miss Mollie again for some time hoping the affair would cool down a little, and rested well contented until a report was out that she had a new suitor, and people said that she leaned up to him like a sick kitten to a hot rock,[3] as though she had never cared anything for me.

It looked hard to a man up a tree, but I consoled myself by recollecting that I knew where the sweetest spot on her face was—on her little pouting lips, I had kissed them often. But this consolation did not last long, for very soon it was rumored in town that Mollie was going to marry him. I grunted mightily, but said nothing. I felt a great rising up and sinking down sensation under my short ribs. I saw every hope vanish. I saw I had to haul to. Yes, farewell, Mollie, I have loved thee too true; but for my foolishness you might have been the one with whom I could have lived—with whom I could have been the happiest of beings. But now the dream is sadly o'er—it is too late—and, down I fell on the bed, and the tears ran out of me like a shower-bath. What shall I do? It is useless to think any more about it now, but I will be revenged yet.

The night was set; preparations were making for a grand festival; and sad, sad the thought that I was to become the object of scorn and ridicule, without being able to retaliate. A short time's reflection opened a way by which I could wreak my vengeance on the heads of my persecutors. Only two days more, and then Miss Mollie was Miss Mollie no more, but Mrs. Koot. Ah! my young man, I'll Koot you, though in doing it I run the risk of inflicting an injury on her who has been the object of my heart's earliest and dearest affections.

Nearly every person in the village was invited, except myself; this I did not expect, or even wish for; I had as much to do that night as I could well attend to. An hour or two before the nuptials were to be served up, I might or may not have been seen sloping off to the woods in search of something.[4] What do you think it was? A limb to hang myself to? No, that wasn't it; all but that It was something that hangs on trees, but it don't grow there; something bigger than a common sized dog's head, but it wasn't that neither. I had seen it hanging to that tree a long time: it was made of a very frail material, collected from fence rails, house tops, &c.; very tender, but strong enough to protect the inmates of a stormy night and cold days; and stout enough to keep them safely housed when you stop the inlet and outlet. I went up carefully and found it as it was when I last saw it; it was hanging to a limb that was near the ground, so I could reach it without any trouble. I had some wads of paper for the purpose of stopping the entrance, and, seeing they were all in, I stopped up the mouth, took out my knife, and soon had all things ready for returning to the scene of action.

I got back to the office in good time; it was getting dark, too much so for any one to notice me with my knapsack. A few minutes and the marriage is to take place. Ah! if it does, it will be at the expense of a good share of suffering to all present.

While I was summing up the cost and the probable result of my intentions, an old negro belonging to the father of Miss Mollie, came by the door of the office. I was standing waiting for the moment to arrive when I should put my plans in execution. Says he to me—

"Wy massa, haint you going to de weddin' at our house?"

"No, Jerry; your old master don't like me, and has not invited me."

"Well, massa, I tells you one ting wat dis nigga knows. Miss Moll don't like dat Koot, but ole massa say she shall hab 'im, cause he no want you to get her."

"Ah! well, Jerry, I can't help it; go on home."

I should have liked very much to talk to Jerry more on the subject, but knew that time was precious at that moment. Now that Jerry was gone, my feelings were horrid in the extreme. I now saw what a game had been played off on me. Mollie, dearest Mollie, she loved me still, and oh! how cruel I had been not to seek an interview with her after my difficulties at her father's— but now the time is past—gone forever. In this state of excitement I shut up my door, took up the bundle, and started to carry out my revenge. I got to the back door as these words were spoken by the *Squire*—

"If any person or persons present has just cause why this man and this woman should not be joined in the holy bonds of matrimony,[5] let them now speak, or forever after hold their peace."

It seemed as if there was an unusual pause after the words were spoken, and now, I thought, was my time to speak in tones of thunder. I pulled out the pieces of paper, and, as I did so, put the mouth of one of the biggest hornet's nests in a crack under the door, that ever you imagined. The little creatures poured out like bees swarming. After I thought they were nearly all out, I grabbed the mouth again, and started for the office with all the power in me. I got in and soon put fire to the hornet's nest.

The office was very close to the old man's house. I went upstairs to see what effect these little insects would have on matrimony or its intention. I had not reached the top of the stairs before I heard some of the most heart-rending screams, the keenest shrieks, the loudest groans that ever fell on mortal ear. The house was crowded with old men and young men, old women and young women, boys, girls, and little children in great abundance. No sooner had the hornets been turned loose than they commenced a regular war on every person in the house. The first one to be assaulted was the old Squire. A whaling big old fellow the size of a bumblebee hauled away and let him have it between the eyes; and still better, Mr. Koot's nose, being the most prominent part about him, except his organ for stealing, was run into worse than a snagged steamboat, and they did not content themselves with his nose, but poked it to every available spot about him. As you might imagine, this soon scattered the crowd, and in time too to save my own dear Mollie from an alliance with that baboon, Koot. There was not another word said after asking if there was any objection to the union, for the end of that pause found the hornets playing *old Harry* with their fair faces.[6] They ran out as if the Devil himself was after them. They knocked down the fences, run over wood-piles, and cut more didoes than a monkey in hot water.[7] They roared like lions, screamed like panthers, yelled worse than Indians, and jumped higher than negroes at a camp-meeting. I enjoyed it, *I did.* One thing strange there was, in the rounds, Miss Mollie did not receive the first injury. After the hornets doing so much in the way of stinging, there could be nothing more done that night. They concluded to put it off until another night; in fact I don't think the Squire or Mr. Koot could have stood still long enough to say two words. The old lady and gentleman were in equally as bad a fix, as well as many others that were present. Violent inflammation set in, and before morning my preceptor was called to see some twenty of them, and I believe Koot was about as bad as any in the mess.

> Fire and tow, here below—
> Ah! fool, look out—I told you so:
> Go home and see your mammy, O!

And she'll learn you how to "skin a tater" or bring a basket of chips to make the soap bile.

CHAPTER VII

A DEATH-BED SCENE

Air—O, leave me to my sorrow.

A hope has lighted up my path
Of happiness in future,
And now, amid the threats and wrath,
My plans at last will conquer;
Hark! the cloud in darkness rises
To burst when o'er my head,
And hope as quickly vanishes,
As I look upon the dead.

MYSELF.

THE wedding of Miss Mollie and Koot was postponed a few days, and I thought I would make one effort to see her again or write to her before another attempt was made, as they would no doubt be on the lookout for intruders. Whether they thought it was me that played the trick on them or not, I am not able to say, but they said nothing to that effect that I ever heard of. There was another heart beside my own, that thrilled with joy, on account of the failure described in the last chapter; it was Miss Mollie. Yes, she would have been willing to suffer more than all the persons present did to escape such a sacrifice, for she hated Koot worse than any man on earth; she told him she did not love him and never could. He saw, though, that her parents would do anything to prevent her from marrying me. I was studying what course to pursue next morning, and picked up my book as usual, and started off to a beautiful woods near the village. I was in the habit of going there every day to study. It was a thick grove of trees between two little hills, and a fine place for study and retirement. I went and sat down on that same old log that had been my seat before, but there was no such thing as studying that morning. I was thinking of the past, present, and future: I blamed myself for my many foolish acts. I could think of no way by which I could ever again speak to her that I loved with all the affection of my youthful heart. I was miserable; my thoughts availed me nothing: my young heart could bear it no longer, I burst into tears. Ah! yes, well do I remember the feelings to-day, as my fragile form gently sank beneath the weight, and I let myself to the ground. My head was resting on the log with my handkerchief over my face; I was in the deepest agony—but list! I hear a sound—I look up, I wipe away my tears, and what do I see? Is it an angel from the realms of bliss above coming to console me? Do my eyes deceive me? No, it must be her. Yes, it is the object of all my thoughts. She approached me. I arose from my situation on the ground and sat upon the log. My heart was beating convulsively. She came up and said to me,

"Why do you thus weep?"

"Ah! Miss Mollie, would that I might say dear Mollie, as once I did, but now I dare not: I have cause to weep: the thought that a few days more and then I must abandon every hope of receiving the sweet smiles of the one that is now before me; the one I love, the one to whom I plighted my affections, is sufficient cause—"

"Dear Doc, don't speak thus, you will break my heart. Do you not know that I saw you leave the office, and thinking you were coming here, I have come to let you know that Mollie loves you yet, and is still willing to be yours, notwithstanding that last night I came near making myself miserable for life, and but for the circumstances that occurred I would have been consigned to a life of wretchedness. My parents have tried to make me marry that unfeeling villain; but now, dear Doc, it is with you to save me from impending danger. Can you still love your own dear Mollie? will you stand by her when persecution arises? will—"

"Come to my arms, my sweet girl; though they be weak, I promise you that by them the mighty shall fall, ere they tear thee from my bosom."

She leaned fondly on me as I imprinted a kiss on her sweet lips. Again she was mine, and mine forever. She said she must hurry back, and what arrangements we had to make, must be done quick. I told her to hold out faithful, and I was ever ready to stand by her. We made arrangements to meet often at the same place, and, after pledging everlasting fidelity to each other, she left.

After she was gone, my poor heart was at ease.

In ten or twelve days after this, her parents told her that the wedding must come off. Now came the trying point, the one that would test her love. It was soon decided. She let all things go on, all arrangements be made as before, told me in the mean time, though, what she intended doing. The night arrived, and all things seemed fast coming to a close. They were again on the floor, the ceremony proceeded until it came to the part, "Will you take this man to be your lawful husband &c.?" When she loosed her arm from his, and said:

"*No, I never will.* I am pledged to another, and I never agreed to marry this man. I was tried to be forced to marry him, but now say in the presence of these witnesses, *I never will marry him.*"

There was great excitement for awhile about it, but finding she would not agree to marry him on any terms, they gave it up. She would not see him again that night after leaving the room. Her parents made use of every means to keep her and I from meeting: we met a few times at the same romantic spot in the woods, but her parents finding that out, it was put a stop to; we passed notes and sweet smiles at each other for a time: this too was detected and prohibited, and soon her parental home was nothing more than a prison to her. Ah, cruel, cruel parents, that could thus trifle with your child's happiness! You know not what you do; you, ere long, will weep over your barbarous triumph. Yes, could it be otherwise? In a short time those rosy cheeks were growing pale, those eyes so bright were soon dimmed by sorrow. It passed unnoticed by her parents, who, seeking nothing else but their own ends to accomplish, let her suffer uncared for until this dear creature was prostrated on a bed of languishing and affliction with cheeks burning with fever. They were at last alarmed, and tried to restore her by kinder treatment; but, ah, the time had passed. The trouble of mind contributed something, in fact was the exciting cause, of her disease; but she would one day have fallen a victim to the disease, which was consumption.[1] She thought, though, that it was altogether the treatment her parents had exercised toward her that caused her sickness, not knowing that she was predisposed to consumption. Medical aid was procured; she was treated a short time by another physician, living in the village, but all to no purpose. My preceptor was then called in consultation; he told her parents she must go in a short time, that nothing could be done for her. As he was going out of the door, my preceptor was told that the young lady wanted to see him alone. He went in, and she said to him—

"Doctor, I feel that I am only going to live a few days; don't deceive me: what do you think of me?"

He told her candidly that he did not think himself that she could.

"Well, then, will you tell Pa and Ma to come here?"

He called them; they came in, and then she talked to them, for the first time, about dying. She said—

"My dear parents, you have made my life a misery to me; deprived me of the society of one that you knew I loved; brought me now near the grave, and the doctor says I can't live many days: will you grant me one request, that I may see Mr. Rattlehead to-day, and every day that I have to live? He loves me; may I see him?"

Those parents, who before had refused her almost every request, told her to ask for anything and it should be granted. How strange that parents will sometimes treat their children so cruel, and yet love them. They do not remember that their children have tender feelings, like they once had themselves. She told the doctor to tell me to come over and see her, that her parents were willing. He came to the office and told me. It was the most welcome news that ever greeted my ear.

I went and oh, what a scene! to see her who, a few weeks before, was a paragon of beauty, now reduced to a shadow. But though she was so feeble, her voice was good, her love was steadfast, her heart was true. I had hardly crossed the threshold of her father's dwelling, when Miss Mollie, poor creature, raised up in her bed and said:—

"My dear Doc, do I see you once more?"

I went to her; I pressed her to my heart; I kissed her pale lips; she again laid down. May God forbid that any of those who may read these pages should ever have to know, by sad experience, my feelings at that moment. I was allowed to visit her until she died which was ten days after I first saw her. The time is past— the scene is o'er: but it will never be forgotten. She died resting on my arm; she died happy. She's gone to rest in heaven.

> Farewell, dear Mollie, I see thee no more,
> Thy trouble and sufferings are now at an end;

"My dear Doc, do I see you once more?"

You're gone to reap your reward in store,
   But you have left to weep a faithful friend.
Years have past since the last fond look
   I took of thee, thou sweetest of beings;
Thou art lying near the murmuring brook
   On which we met in by-gone days.

Often memory will bring back
   A thought of where you now repose,
And oh! how sweet 't will be to think
   Thy soul no sorrow knows.
Farewell to the spot, it's long since faded
   From my vision, then so bright,
But will be cherished and regarded
   With remembrance never dying.

CHAPTER VIII

A NEW PLAN
FOR CATCHING A ROGUE

Air—Good-by, you've broke my head.

When winter comes with chilling frost
We know the summer's gone,
And quick to work, no time is lost,
We gather in our corn.
But something else we know we want,
Besides this common food,
Houses tight to keep us in,
And good supply of wood.

CORKSCREW.

As may well be supposed, after passing through so many sore trials, I could not study much for several days. The thought, though, that Miss Mollie loved me to the last expiring moment, and that she had escaped a life of misery, by not marrying the man she could not love, was one consoling thought that made me better prepared to stand the shock. I knew that she was happy. I knew that weeping for her would not bring her back, would not make me any more happy in future. Before long I recovered from the effects of it, and commenced studying again.

It was not getting cold weather, and I confined myself to the office very closely. I had a fine lot of wood laid up for the winter, and thought now that my life would be a comparatively smooth one to what it had been for a few months past. I had no more love-scrapes, no more "negro stealing," nothing now to interrupt me. I was imbibing knowledge very fast, comfortably seated by a good wood fire from early morn until late at night. I had but little to say to any person but my preceptor. I often felt gloomy and sad in reflecting over the many unpleasant scenes of the past, the solitude of the present, and fears of the future. Notwithstanding my retired life it was not so much so but that I could discover any injury or injustice done me from any source whatever. I observed that my stock of wood, which I had thought quite ample for the season, was fast melting away. I thought I was not extravagant in the use of it myself; could it be that any person in the village was so friendly with me as to "take a little" of a cold morning before I got out of bed? I did not know of any one so remarkably intimate with me as that, but the fact was, the wood was going too fast, and I was determined to see how it was. I had some pieces cut of a suitable length for putting on the fire, and left them outside of the door. Next morning the wood was gone. I tried the experiment the second time; the result was the same. I had now fairly tested the matter, and found that some person was toating[1] it off: but now who did it, was the question, and how was I to find it out; and more important still how to put a stop to it. It was too cold to stand out and watch, and besides that, I had something else to do, and no time to spare. I wanted to put a stop to such an infringement on my rights; how was I to do it? I was puzzled no little about it, but finally a plan occurred to me that I thought would meet the exigencies of the case. There were some knotty old beeches that were hard to split, and not very valuable, that I had cut of the usual length for putting on the fire, took them into the office and bored two or three holes in each piece with an auger, about halfway through them. I then took some gunpowder, filled the holes half full of it, then fitted tight wooden pins to put into them, making a small groove on the side of the pins, by which I could fix a match, the external part to be filled with cotton, wadded in to prevent the powder from running out until the wood was on the fire. I put these out at the back door, as previously. I did not sit up very late that night, but retired to bed, hoping that before another sun should rise I should be waked up by the sound of "gunpowder on fire in a tight place."

I was resting from the labors of the day, and dreaming very interestingly on some medical subject, when I was awakened by the sound of something in the upper part of the village. There was more than half a dozen slapbangs—roaring like fifty-sixes well charged.[2] I got up as easy[3] as I could and went to the window to see if I could tell anything of where it was. I heard a mighty noise like people running, brush cracking, children crying, men groaning, women screaming, horses neighing and running in every direction. Such a noise could not fail to arouse the good people of that quiet little place from their lethargy. I concluded to be in the fashion, and got up too, to see what was the consequence. I began to fear that I had done a horrid deed for the sake of saving a little wood; but no time to think of that part of the job now it was done. I dressed myself as soon as I could, and went up to behold the effect of wood-stealing.

Reader, were you ever present when a steamboat exploded, or a steam-car ran off the track down a big bluff? If so, you can form some idea of what a picture presented itself when I went up. It was something remarkable that, on that very night there was a little "coming together" of some of the young people of the village, to have a bit of fun in the way of dancing, playing, &c. It is now long since the circumstance I am giving you an account of occurred, but I almost shrink from the task as I attempt to pen it for your reading to-day; such an impression was there made on me at that moment. I *almost* repented that I had acted so harshly for such a trivial cause, but I recollected it was my lot always to be in scrapes, and was reconciling it to my own feelings the best I could. I felt pretty safe as regarded the law, for they would not dare to speak of it even, or censure me in any way.

Well, I must get through with this. I am taking up time and space telling you of my feelings, and have neglected to finish the history of the case. As I said, I went in and found many persons there besides those that were invited to the party. The noise had awakened many "that slept," and they came to see what was on hand. Where do you suppose this party and my wood was at, and who was there? It was at the house of one Mr. Koot. "It wasn't anywhere else." You recollect Koot, don't you? Yes, my rival. I thought you did. I'll tell you all how it happened.

You see this Koot and I didn't like one another better than a dog likes hickory, anyway, and he thought, to vex me a little, he would steal my wood; and, still more to wound my pride, his father gave a little party to *his particular* friends, and left my friends and me with "the bag to hold."[4] (Very glad he did.) When they all got in a good way, John Koot, the young man, sent or come himself, I don't care which, all the same, you know and waged[5] off my wood, all ready for putting on the fire—quite convenient, you see, (all bored and full of powder, if he'd known it,) and carried it up and laid it on the fire—cold night, very good thing in its place. All was proceeding well, and doubtless they were exulting over me, when one of *Amos Jackson's* baby-wakers[6] burst loose in all its power. It told a tale of bloodshed and broken noses never to be forgotten. I went in, and as bad as I was at tricks, I felt greatly mortified that I had done as I did. It had played dreadful havoc indeed. The old man Koot, poor fellow, was the first I observed. A piece of the log had struck him just above the knee, his leg was badly bruised and torn, and was bleeding like a spring sprout.[7] Young Koot—unhappy man, I feel for you to this day— had the worst injury of anyone in the room. His skull was badly fractured, and he was lying on the floor perfectly senseless, and the blood gushing from the wound in torrents. The old lady, Mrs. Koot, happened to be in another room, and was not hurt. Miss Koot, though she was as ugly as a mud fence,[8] I could but feel sorry for her. Her arm was fractured above the wrist. Many others were injured slightly, such as broken noses, splinters of wood in the back, and other things too tedious to mention.

Mercy save us! the old woman was making more noise than I ever heard proceed from mortal lips. She out-squalled an Indian, knocked her hands together worse than a rattle-trap, jumped higher than a dog in an oat patch,[9] shook like an earthquake, fell up and got down faster than a fool on ice,[10] and made more motions than a calf choked with a hemp rope three feet down its throat.

Medical aid was procured as soon as possible, and as there was no other physician to be found in the place but my preceptor, he was called. It was a fine job for him, and I too, as I assisted in dressing the wounded; and before day we had them all in as good condition as could be expected. Young Koot had a dangerous fracture; we took out a piece of the bone, which soon restored him to consciousness, and eventually he recovered; in fact they all got well without any trouble, except paying the doctor-bill. It was a profitable job for my preceptor; he got a very decent sum for his services. As I had prognosticated, there was no fuss made about the affair in any way by the Koot family; it was too plain they had been stealing wood.

In a short time after this, the family, all in a lump by themselves, picked up their *duds* and left our parts—and have not been heard of since; and if this little volume should ever fall into their hands, or their hands should ever fall on this volume, I hope they will pardon me for naming the circumstances.[11] I have started out to give my readers my life a little in detail, and could not do justice to them and leave it out of my book. I did not lose any more wood that winter, *I didn't*. In conclusion, let me say to those that lose wood "Go and do likewise."

CHAPTER IX

BLOODSHED AND HYSTERICS

Air—Here blood as free as water flows.

A lady and daughter one morn did come
A distance of three miles from home;
It was to see an older doc. than I
A string around their arm to tie.
"Madam, him you can not find,
But I am here to treat you kind."
"Mother, now *let him pierce my vein,*
And that will take away my pain."

SALLY HOOKER.

Thus ended my difficulties for awhile. I found that unless I quit such tricks as I had been at all my life, I would kill somebody, and I did not want to do that; I had been in scrapes enough; I had become tired of it. I had been reading for some time without any trouble with mankind and human beings in general, and considered quite a change had come over the "spirit of my dreams." Actuated by these feelings, I thought it high time that I was doing something to make people believe I was learning to be a doctor. There were many chronic cases that came to the office to be prescribed for. So, not to put the doctor to so much trouble going to see them—and many of them I knew were not danger-ous—why can't I try my luck on them? I can do as well perhaps, as the old doctor in many of those cases.

One morning an old lady and her daughter called at the office to be bled. Many persons in that part of the country were in the habit of being bled once a year; it was an old custom, and it is a vulgar notion, I have been informed, of many persons, even to this day, in the highest circles of society.[1] My preceptor was out, visiting some patients. The old lady, after telling me the object of her visit, asked where the old doctor was. I informed her that he was absent, and would not return for some hours; but, says I, if you only want to be bled, I can do that for you as well as the old doctor or anybody else.

"You look like bleeding anyone, don't you? You don't know enough to bleed my old bay mare that's with colt in the rye-patch."

"Oh hush, ma'am," says the young lady; "I reckon young doc-tors has got some sense as well as old ones."

"Well, I s'poses you think so," replied the old lady.

"Yes, I am willing to let him *try on me*, if he has ever bled any-body before—have you ever done the like?"

"Madam, if I have bled one person, I have bled a thousand; besides, I have been in this office more than a year hard at study, reading medical books, and improving every day."

"Oh, well, Sally, do as you please. I believe you like the young men best, anyhow."

By thus evading the question, I soon had a case. I got out my lancet that the old doc. had given me, and flourished it round in a wise manner, like I had bled somebody before: well, I had, but not with the lancet exactly—remarking at the same time that bleeding was a small affair. Bandage, bowl, staff, &c., all being ready I laid hold of as fat and plump an arm as ever hung from the body of a damsel since Adam. I took up the bandage to cord her arm, and not knowing anything about how tight it should be, drew it round like a bear hugging a dog—so close it couldn't breathe.

"Oh! mercy help me, you will cut off my arm, doctor."

"Not by any means, my dear lady; I was just trying to see how tight you could bear it; some persons, you know, must have a bandage much tighter than others. I suppose you must be a little on the nervous order."

This the old lady objected to, saying that "Sally had never been 'sterical in her life."

I had to ease her mind on that point before proceeding further, and this I did by telling her that I meant nothing about hysterics; I meant that her daughter's sensitiveness only proved that she was more refined in her feelings than most of ladies.

"I thought so; she's a very smart girl, doctor."

I relaxed the bandage a little, and now for the worst part of it. I was scared awful, but I was in for a trial then. I made a lick at the arm with the lancet, and happened to strike the vein. The blood run quite free, and the old lady was praising me for my skill, for such a short study, until I concluded Sally had bled enough. I loosed the bandage, and not knowing more about the process, I was standing there thinking how to stop the blood. The young lady was still bleeding as fast as ever, from the fact that she let her hand and arm swing down for the blood to run off of her fingers instead of on her dress. The old lady was getting alarmed for her daughter's safety. Sally commenced crying; still the blood run. The old lady, not knowing what else to do tore off her bonnet, made an attempt to hollow[2] for help and, failing to do this, she fell down in a fit of hysterics. Now, my feller mortals, you see the condition of affairs, how do you feel? I don't know how you feel, or would have felt, had you been in my situation, but I felt with my fingers.[3]

When the old lady concluded to take the hysterics Sally grew much worse, and keeled over with a fainting fit, or rather, she was suffering from too great an "afflux of blood to the arm." I had often thought I was in a scrape before, in life, and doubtless you may think I had been, but now I could have got all my scrapes together in a bag, and this would take the rag off your noses; in fact it was the scrapings of creation.[4] To think of it was enough to make the blood run hot in my toe nails. Just think of it. I don't believe you are half as much interested in it as I ever was in anything in my life; the old lady lying there on the floor, foaming at the mouth, and gasping for breath, or a little water, I didn't know which; Sally, a beautiful girl of fifteen, with pale countenance and fluttering pulse, seemed in the last agonies of death, lying at my feet. Ah! horror of horrors, and my old hat for a bee-gum! did I ever think such was to be my fate in life, after all the danger and bloodshed through which I had passed! Farewell to every fond hope and bright expectation, that had once lighted up my path. Here now lay the work of my hands; two innocent females consigned to a premature grave by my presumption; a husband—a father, made miserable by my heedlessness, my unguarded actions. I wish you to bear in mind, though, my friends, that I did not take as much time on that occasion to do something, as I have on this page to do nothing.

You may judge I was for looking to the young lady first, as my preceptor had always told me to remove the cause and the effect would cease. I reasoned thus: as Sally's bleeding caused the old lady to take the hysterics, I must staunch the blood before either would be relieved; good syndesmology,[5] wasn't it; but, like many others in medical science, very absurd in the abstract. Well, think as you please, I acted accordingly, and now for the result. I looked at Miss Sally's arm and found that it had quit bleeding—a very natural result—when she fainted, a small clot formed, and stopped up the orifice. I took advantage of the auspicious moment, and put a piece of cotton over the orifice, and a bandage. I then put ammonia to her nostrils, threw cold water in her face and the dear little creature opened her eyes, drew her breath fast for a few moments, and before long was on her feet trying to revive her mother. She asked me for some spirits of camphor, saying her ma'am must always have it when she was in that fix. The camphor soon had the desired effect; the old lady bounced up and commenced a terrible squall about the way I had done, but soon quit it, when I told her if she would say nothing more about it I would not charge her anything, and come to see Sally three times a week in the bargain. This soon made us friends, and if ever the scrape leaked out, you have my mouth for a wash-bowl. I'll tell you the reason; as I said before, I promised to go and see Sally three times a week, merely to keep peace in the family.

A week or two after the "venesection"[6] of Sally, I strolled over to see her, only three miles off, but in one of the most pugliferous, agroomenous, ambiguous, cadaverous, sudorloric "Hollows"[7] that you ever did see. I rode up as authoritative as a sheep to a haystack, got off my horse and went in. I arrived in the best time, perhaps, for as soon as I reached the door the old lady bawled out—

"Polkstalks and leather breeches! there comes our ramstuginous little doctor; how are you?"[8]

"Very well, madam, I thank you, hope I find you and family well?"

"Most awful well since our spree in town the other day. I won't tell anybody 'bout it, though, you know. Look here, Doc., Sal was never so well in all her life; I believe she is puttier than ever I was when I was a gal in ole Virginny; but I'll go and bring her out, though, and you can judge for yourself."

And so saying she put off into the other cabin for Sally. I was thinking, "Well, old woman, if you think to put your daughter off on me, you are as bad mistaken as if you had burnt your shirt; not because she is not pretty, but I can't forget my dear Mollie so soon as this; and besides this, I don't want to marry nohow up in these hollows."

In she come, before I got done thinking, with Sally, blushing like a millstone.[9] She had improved very much. The old lady said to me that they were going to have a frolic there that night, and was glad I had come.[10] She said she had sent Bill over for old Pat Dismukes, and he would soon be back with the fiddle, and then we would have some fun; "I think we deserve a little after all of us coming so near losing our reputation, or our lives, you know, about the same thing. I haint[11] told 'bout that yet, though, an' aint goin' to."

I had a great time with Sally, about how she looked when she fainted. I told her she looked so white and nice about the lips, I felt like kissing her.

"I wish you had, it would soon brought me to my right feelings."

But, making short of a long story, Bill did soon come back with the fiddler, and then they commenced, and "frog ponds and old newspapers!" what a row they kept up for three or four hours. As Sally and I didn't dance, we set off in one corner and talked most tarnal agreeable all the time. At last they all feared they might wear out their new shoes, and was about breaking up when an unexpected, unnatural, unabridged circumstance occurred. The old man and old woman got to talking very loud about the pigs rootin up the taters, and we all concluded to stay and see the fun outside in, if there was any more.[12] The evil spirit had been in and among the crowd during the evening, and was now doing its share of good. They kept quarrelling until their labial prolongations made as much noise as the bolt of a wheat mill. So much labor was not to be lost. The old man plainly told her, if she did not hush he would frail her worse than a dog would a polecat.[13] She was not disposed to bear any encroachment on her rights or her lefts either, and therefore gathered the broomstick and commenced giving him a good sweeping. He closed in on her, and they commenced a regular "buster." The persons present didn't touch or say a word, and they continued uninterrupted until she got two or three inches of the old man's nose between her teeth. This is more than any man can stand, so he bawled out like something hurt him. They were soon separated, but too late to save the old man's nose. She had taken an inch or so for breakfast. When she saw what was done, she gave one keen "Oh, ma!" and down she came, with a fit of hysterics, coflumpux on the floor.[14]

What a fortunate thing I happened to be here to-night. I'll get a case of surgery, and I did too. Without saying a word to any person present, whether they desired my services or not, I took the piece of nose from the old lady's mouth and put it in situ[15] on the old man. I could not help thinking how much he looked like a big fat bull pup, before the end of his nose was put on. I got a needle and thread and sowed it on the best I could, and then, by taking the white of an egg for plaster, I completed the dressing. By this time someone had aroused the old lady.

Thus ended the frolic in the little hog-skin hollow. But my name was soon sounded far and near as a surgeon. The old man's nose growed on again fast; yes it did, you needn't be contending about whether it could or not.

But now good night; the wolves are howling most beautifully out on the bayou, and I can sleep so much better by some such music as that. I know you will excuse me until morning, and then commences another chapter.

CHAPTER X

AQUA FORTIS AND CROTON OIL, OR TAKING THE WRONG MEDICINE

Air—Stop dat kicking.[1]

Haste! doctor, haste! to save my son,
Or he must quickly die;
A horse in fright has caused a stun
That made his mammy cry.
With head and tail raised in the air
We start to see the splutter;
But 'fore we safely landed there
We found we'd lost the butter.

OLE PADDY.

AFTER taking a good meal of venison this morning, I am again prepared to proceed with my history; and let me here state that I will not pretend to give a full history of my life; it would require a much larger volume than you have patience to read, or I have time to write. I only give you an account of incidents as I can now recollect them. I write entirely from memory, and give such as I think will amuse and instruct. At no very remote period,

should this little volume meet with public favor, I expect to prepare another that will, I trust, be equally if not more edifying
than the present one.[2] I recollect many scenes, that I have no
doubt would prove highly amusing, that occurred during the re-
mainder of my studies, but I will pass them all by until we arrive
near the close of my studies in the office of my preceptor. This
will be a short account of the first case that I was bold enough
to take the responsibility of mounting my steed and throwing
across his back a pair of saddle-bags; not a regular pair of physicians' saddle-bags, but a pair of ordinary saddle-bags that would
hold near half a bushel. One day about ten o'clock, a man came
riding into the village like streaks of blue lightning were after
him, without shoes or coat, and a rope bridle, without any saddle
or blanket, bawling at the top of his head—

"Doctor, doctor, run here, my son will die! for God's sake
run here!"

Ever and anon I was on the look *in* for a chance to do some
good for my friends and particular acquaintances, especially in
that part of our country, through my neighborhood and section.
He rode up to the office and called out for the old doctor. I told
him he was not at home. He then asked if there was any other
doctor in the place. I told him there was none at home but myself.

"What! are you a doctor?"

"Well, now, that's a nice question to ask, indeed; what do you
think I would be doing in the office, if I wasn't a doctor?"

"Well," said he, "get your horse as soon as possible, or sooner,
if possible, for my son is very bad."

I asked him what was the matter; he told me his son had been
badly hurt by a fall from his horse. I told him to get down and
wait a few moments, and I would be ready. He did so, and I had
my horse ready in a short time, but then I was in a fix to know
how to carry some medicines with me. I was well aware, that unless I took some few medicines along I would not make a good
impression. I happened to look under the counter and saw a pair

of saddle-bags, such as persons in the country are in the habit of taking along when they travel. I did not want to let the old fellow see me fixing up, lest he should smell a rat, or some assafoetida. I asked him to walk in the back room, if he pleased, until I was ready. He did so, and then I commenced filling up. I scarcely know now what I didn't put in, but among others, I recollect the following:—Calomel, 1 lb.;³ jalap, ½ lb; ipecac (jar), 8 oz; croton oil, 1 bottle; salts, 2 pounds; 2 big gimlets; 1 large carving knife; 4 yds of canvas for bandages; 1 paper pins; 1 lb mustard; 6 cupping glasses;⁴ 1 pr. toothpullers; 1 pint (bottle) aqua ammonia; 2 yds adhesive plaster, and many other articles too tedious to mention, making in all enough to fill both ends of the saddle bags.

"Halloo, my old friend, all ready now, let us be off."

He came out and looked at the saddle-bags mighty hard for a little while, but said nothing. Fearing he might be displeased with my appearance, as a doctor, I remarked to him that he must excuse me for carrying such a large pair of saddle-bags, it was all for the good of my patients. Says I, "Sir, I am not like most of your proud fops of doctors, who take a little pair of bags about large enough to hold a half dozen two-ounce vials, and when they get to their patients, have to send back home for medicines, and while they are about it their patients might die. I take medicine enough to do some good and I am not too proud to carry a large pair."

Oh, Mol! what an impression that made on him; you could see the in-tent-a-sham on his skin. The large quantities of medicine that I put in was not so much a matter of choice as necessity. I had no time to tarry for etiquette then. All things looking favorable, we started; yes, we started to get there in a minute. We put our horses out at their level best, and, as I had rather the best one of the two, I kept before. I could see persons looking at me as I went on, as though they could not believe it was me. The old man lived five or six miles off and before we reached there our horses as well as ourselves were hauling sail.⁵ We were riding along talking very busily, and I suppose the old man thought, very learnedly, when my horse began to sidle to the left like a steamboat going to land stern foremost. He switched his tail, he humped his back, he snorted, he kicked, he reared up, and cut more shines than a snapping-turtle on hot iron.[6]

"What is the matter?" says the old man, "is there yellow-jackets about?"

We commenced looking as well as we could, but found no cause for such unqualified objections to my situation on his dorsal ridge. He got worse and worse, and soon at that point where a man had better stay on than get off. Not knowing what else to do he broke like he was scared to death for the woods. He went rolling equal to wildfire over logs, rocks, bushes, briers, and such other things as came in his way. He did not keep up his efforts long until he walloped me as slick as soap on the ground. I soon found out what the poor animal was making all this complaint about, for in my fall the saddle-bags were thrown all in a lump on me, striking about fifteen inches above my knees, and me flat on my face. I felt a little of the awfulest, warmest, keenest, hottest, gnawin'est, burnin'est, peculiarest, unpleasantest sensation that ever crawled over a man's "glutei" in Christendom.[7] I put my hand round to see if I was on fire, and the same action was set up on my manual extremity. By this time the old man came up. I asked him to look at the saddle-bags and see if any of the medicine had leaked out. He turned them over, and if they wasn't as black as my hat, you may swallow me. What could be in the saddle-bags of such a corrosive nature? He commenced, and the first bottle he took out was labeled *Aqua Fortis,* instead of *Aqua Ammonia,* as I took it to be in my haste at the office.[8] The aqua fortis bottle had lost its stopper out, and it leaked out through the leather on the horse's back. I told the old man to get me some water, if possible. There was a spring near by, and he went and brought me his hat full, as this was all he had to bring it in. I washed off my horse the best I could, and did not forget myself

either. Having fixed up all things, we again set out to see the sick
patient. We arrived there very soon, and found the young man
lying on a bed in a state of stupefaction, with the following
symptoms: laborious breathing, eyes closed, pulse full and heavy,
and, the old woman sitting in the chimney-corner crying like she
was fond of it. I went to the bed, took him by the hand and tried
to rouse him. It was all no go, he only "uh-ha-hi-oc"—and that
was the amount of information I could get about his case. I
fumbled round him for awhile, doctor like, and told the family
that I hoped I could restore him in an hour or two. I went to the
saddle-bags to see if something useful would not present itself.

"Potato pies, brickbats, and old shoes! if ever you saw such a
muss, you may larap me two hours with a cow's tail." I pulled
out, and pulled out, until I had got near everything in them on
the floor, and not a piece of medicine as big as a hickory-nut of
one kind could be found without being mixed with another except the vial of croton oil. This was my only resource, and it was
the very thing, I thought, for I recollected of reading that it was
used in concussion and compression of the brain. I uncorked it,
poured out half a teaspoonful, got some molasses, *mixed well together,* and poured it into the patient's mouth as he lay on his
back. As it happened, his throat opened a little, and down it went.
I told the old man it would operate, I thought in an hour or two;
sat down, and commenced thinking over the case and the medicine. I did not think long until I thought I had given him a deadly
dose, for, instead of half a teaspoonful being a dose, from one to
two drops was sufficient, and an old saying was, it always killed
or cured.[9]

Father of big-rabbits, and door-sill of Bell Towers! what must I
do? I kept thinking on the affair, and noticing the patient for half
an hour, when I was awakened to a sense of do something, by
this potent drug displaying its effects on the young man's sen-
for-sum cum-under-me, (sensorium commune.)[10] He raised up
and made out of that house as fast as if forty panthers were after

him. As regards the effects of the medicine, you may have your own way of thinking. Suffice it to say, that the matter of the young man's being thrown from his horse was all a hoax, for there was nothing the matter with him, only "he was drunk." I never let the old man know any better than the notion he entertained of his son's getting thrown from his horse, and in doing that I secured his good feeling; and Joe, the young man told me if I would say nothing about it, he would sign the temperance pledge. I agreed to it. The old man still thinks I worked wonders in a short time, and is one of my warmest friends. Joe is now a son of temperance and has a wife and seven children.

CHAPTER XI

THREE SCRAPES
IN ONE NIGHT

Air—Could I mend my leg again.

Here we have facts in multiplicity,
From greatest sorrow to felicity,
And each in turn has been the lot
(Whether they've told it yet or not),
Of all of Adam's fallen race,
Since he from shame did hide his face.
Now, if any of you want to grumble,
Come down and we will have a tumble.

BANDY SHANKS.

I SHOULD like very much to tell you of some other scrapes that I had while I was with my preceptor, but I have now taken up as much space in that, as the limits of the present volume will admit. I must therefore pass over many things that would be interesting, to allow me more room to describe my adventures after becoming a practitioner in the backwoods of Arkansas. I had been studying two years, and now it was time for me to attend my first course of lectures. I bade adieu to all my old associates, parents, brothers, sisters, and friends, and left for one of the cities in the Western States, to complete my medical education. After all the toil and difficulties attendant on traveling in the States where internal improvements are limited, I arrived at my place of destination. I felt very green when I got to the city and paid dear enough to learn a little of the city ways. I stopped for a day or two at the hotel, until I could find a private boarding house. After getting quiet at the hotel, my next business was to find the Medical College. I found no difficulty in doing this; went in, and there I saw a list of boarding houses as long as the moral laws. I struck out, and after many long talks with the landladies about good board, high rents, dear provisions, coal hard to get, wearing out carpets, good attention if you get sick, comforts of a home, what church do you belong to? that's the one I attend; my boarders never leave me, I thought I would take a few this winter for company; my daughters play well on the piano; nice beds; I think I would like you; nice looking gentleman; widow woman;[1] hard time to get along; just about pay expenses, &c. &c. I procured a situation that I thought I should like, and moved to it. There were five other students boarding in the same house. The old lady was very attentive at first, indeed; kept a good table, and everything went on well. We had been there three weeks, when things began to have a different aspect. The butter was old and rancid; cold biscuit; no meat for supper; weak tea, with plenty of water in it; bad coffee, and all those little things that are usually met with at boarding houses. I waited several days for some of the boys to say something to the lady, but they were from home, like myself, and concluded to grin and endure it;[2] and besides this, when anything was to be done or said, Rattlehead was the one, and they were looking anxiously at me for a start. I was getting tired of such treatment, and could stand it no longer. I went down and made sharp complaint to the landlady. She made many fair promises, and did improve very much on what it had been, and to make the affair pass off the better, fearing she might lose her nice single gentlemen, she gave us a party. Well, the night for it came on, and the boys talked considerable about it, and wanted to know if it was different from our frolics in the country. One of us knew about as much about it as the other, as all of us were from the dry diggins.[3] "We were not in the habit of saying party," in our own circles of society. The following conflameration in the way of a dialogue, took place amongst us six. I will not give any other than the nicknames by which each of us passed; should any of them see this book, they will call to mind our old familiar names. They all called me Lord Byron, from the fact that I was fond of poetry, and occasionally would let a verse leak out of my cranium.

Granser.—"See here, boys, Mrs. Palon is going to give us what she calls a party, to-night; what do you all think of it?"

Old Cow.—"Well, I don't exactly know whether I understand what she means by it; I reckon its some new fashion from New York."

Big Hoss.—"I will tell you all about it. I have seen it out in Indianny, a heap of times; the way they do, they kach a big yallar cat and tie a beef's bladder to his tail, and he runs most awful, till somebody jumps on the bladder and bursts it, and it makes a twerible noise, and—"

Pie Crust.—"Ha! ha! ha! now, Big Hoss, don't tell us anything about how they do things out in Indianny that backwoods country and forest; you never saw anything out there like they do among civilized people."

Parson.—"You all think you know what is coming off, but you don't, and you won't know which end is up when you get in the parlor with these city ladies."[4]

Lord Byron.—"Gentlemen, hold your tongues; you will see one thing; I'll do just as I do when we have a frolic in the country, and if anybody says a word about it, I'll knock him into eternity before he can repeat it."

It might have continued much longer but for my timely inter-
ference. Night came on, and we all were reminded that the trying
moment had come, by the sound of music in the parlor. I never
saw such a set of fools in my life as there was on that occasion;
one would start, then he'd come back; another swore he had palpitation of the heart. Parson had the headache; Old Cow was sick
at the stomach; Pie Crust had to answer a letter; and here they
stood like so many fools at a still-house, until I got tired of such
faint-heartedness, and was as mad as a wet hen.[5] Says I, "You
low-bred, stupid beasts of burthen, if you don't clear out of here
and go down stairs, I'll cut your medical throats. Who's there to
hurt you? a few young ladies with pretty faces. What harm can
they do? If any of them laugh at one in this crowd except old
Indianny, I'll make their countenances hurt them as certain as
you are all fools. As for Big Hoss, he knows all about it, he says;
we'll see very soon." I led the way, they all followed, puffing and
blowing like they had been running a foot race. We were introduced as we went in, and took seats; old Indianny was the last
one to get in and he was so much scared, he sidled off to one side
of the room like he wanted to hide himself. I didn't blame him for
it, for he came down to the parlor, Hoosier fashion in his shirt
sleeves.[6] As he was making off to get out of the way, he ran
against a table and over it went. There was a lamp on the table,
filled with camphene;[7] it fell on the floor, and I rather suppose
you can tell what happened. It gave one little pu, and then it exploded. Poor Indianny was stooping to catch the table before it
fell, but alas! too late. The pieces of glass were thrown in every
direction. He was badly damaged; a piece of glass struck him just
above the left eye and made a severe wound; another piece was
driven into the fleshy part of his shoulder. A piece struck "Old
Cow" on the side of his head, and came near knocking his senses
out; almost every one present was injured more or less; even
your humble servant shared his part this time, and if you ever
come through my neighborhood, please to stop, and I'll show

you on my left hand the marks of that night's fun. Old Indianny was badly burned, besides his other injuries. The lamp was not so large but that it might have been larger, and if it had, it would have put a stop to some of our breathing. There was a blaze of fire as big as an elephant in a minute, and before it could be extinguished the carpet was a gone case. The fire being out, Indianny was to be attended to. We soon had him dressed and comfortable in bed. All persons belonging to the party remained until the fire was out and things quiet. The landlady made a considerable squall for a little while; but finding that did no good, she concluded to say nothing more about it, and proposed that the dance go on. All hands were in for it, and, the back parlor being arranged, we were all ready. A young lady seated herself at the piano and commenced. The old lady cried out, "Partners, gentlemen."

I tell you I felt sort of down in the mouth,[8] because I had never danced a lick in my life. Somehow, or somehow else, they could not get enough to start a set unless I would come in. Old Cow, Granser, and Pie Crust could all dance a little, but I never had attempted it. I did not want to go out there to show my ignorance in a crowd, and still I wanted to dance. I knew that I was in a bad fix with my hand badly cut, to dance, even if I knew how, and I recollected I had went at so many things that I knew nothing about, and paid so dearly for it, that I feared to attempt dancing, not knowing what accident might happen. They were all trying to get me out, anyhow, and said they only wanted me to go through the figures to make out the set. I concluded that they would overlook any awkwardness I might display, and finally agreed to try it. I was introduced to a beautiful young lady; begged the pleasure of dancing with her; she agreed: more, I supposed, to see some fun out of me than anything else. After we were on the floor I told her that I had never danced, and hoped she would bear with me through the set. She said she would make every allowance. It came to our time to go through, and I did make out to walk the rounds, and that was all. My partner praised me very much, and said I did much better than she could expect for the first time. That set being through, I felt much relieved, but still I had to come on the floor every set, now, as I had commenced. I did improve a little, I believe myself, but not as much as I then thought, and as you will think before the scene closes. Look out now what I tell you. We went on until the third or fourth set, and I thought I was "some pumpkins"[9] at dancing. The gentleman that acted as director, cried out something, and we all commenced going round and round, holding to each other's hands. I was as large as anybody, and in one of my attempts to show off a little extra, I did it. As we were going round I made a wrong step, and put my foundation of pedestral existence on the dainty little foot of the young lady that I was dancing with, and—ca-ge-ra-eh-whee—allap! her and I came flat on the floor. She gave one loud scream, and that was the last opportunity she had to say anything, for the others coming round, stumbled over us, and so on in rotation, until everyone was in a confused pile. Such scrambling, hollowing, crying, bleating, laughing, twisting, and rolling over I never heard talk of. We all managed to get upon our feet again, except the young lady that was dancing with "Granser." She was lying on the floor when the others got up, screaming with all her power—

"My arm, my arm! it is broke, it is broke!"

Mutations of man's happiness, and ferry-boats of future pleasures, what have I done now! *another scrape*—I thought so. The young lady was taken up and her arm examined. It was found to be a dislocation of the shoulder joint. I felt a little of the queerest, awfulest, badest, and most squeamish in general; the smallest, longest, awkwardest, and quadrilateral in particular, that a poor wretch ever did in creation. I began to think it was a dear party. The young lady's arm was soon set, but the thought of having given pain to a dear creature like she was, made me feel all overish. I offered my apology by telling them that they had overruled my feelings in the commencement; I was only dancing to oblige them, at the same time remarking that no man could feel a more heartfelt sorrow for the young lady than myself; and as a proof of my sympathy, the doctor's bill should cost her nothing (I set the arm myself, I did, first thing I thought of.) The excitement gradually wore off, and we were about to break up, when the subject of ether was named by some one present. They had all heard of the wonderful effects of this medicine when taken by different individuals, how it showed the disposition of any person, and how strange they acted. They tried every student in the house to get them to take it, except myself, but they declined, as they had never used it. The young lady that had been so unfortunate as to have her shoulder dislocated by my awkwardness, remarked to me in the sweetest tones possible, that if I would take the ether she would forgive me for all past offenses, and smile on me in future. I could not stand such a banter. I said to the young men (the students) that if I took the medicine they must pay for any damage that might result from it. "Certainly," said they.

I took this precaution, because I had heard so much of what persons would do while under its influence, and also because I never went at anything in my life but some accident occurred. I had come near killing several persons in my life, and I was getting cautious. I didn't know what influence the ether would have on me, as I had never taken it. Some of the precious liquid was procured, and all things being ready, I sat down to inhale it. I took it gradually, and well do I remember yet how I felt. I felt some of the biggest sensations that ever crawled over my mortal frame: it seemed as though I could tear down houses, pull up trees, and lick an elephant. My ears trembled like an earthquake, and slowly the sound increased as the anesthetic agent was taken into my system; bu—eh—bu—eh—bu—eh—bu—ah! and I was gone, insensible to all the outward world, and surrounding objects *in general.* How long I was in this situation I can not tell, but when I had a return of consciousness, I know one thing: I had a gash two inches long on the back of my head, and bleeding like a hog, and still more I remember, everybody had left the room in a fright, the old lady hollowing "help! help!" the piano turned heels upward, knocked into twenty pieces and "Old Cow" with his foot mashed as flat as a pancake.[10]

Gentlemen, you remember I have told you there never was a man that got into as many scrapes as I have in life. Only think of it,—two accidents in one night, besides what old Indianny did for a beginning. Old Cow and myself having been dressed, it was moved and seconded, that we adjourn *sine die.*[11] I laid it on the boys in the way of damages, don't you think I did? Nothing more at present, only remain, mine and yours together, when we get there.

CHAPTER XII

A THUNDER STORM, AND
A NIGHT IN THE WOODS

Air—Bull-frog's meditation.

Farewell, old building, I leave you now
To steer my course alone—
You go to the frog-pond
And I'll mind my business—
The lightnings flash, the thunders roar
As they were never heard before—
Musquitoes, wolves, and panthers,
Watch how you make your banters.

DICK HAMESTRING.

WELL, now, I have got through some other difficulties, temptations and trials. What will be next? We all recovered from the injuries received on the eventful night of the "party." The young men were as good as their word: they paid the damage done to the piano, and therefore the landlady could say nothing to me about it. The lady did not keep her good table long, and finding that we could not have such things as we wanted without very great trouble, we concluded to move, and did so. After moving, we had no cause to complain, as we had a fine boarding house.

There were many things that occurred during my stay in that city that I would delight in giving you an account of, but I find I can not do so without crowding out things that relate more especially to the hairbreadth escapes, sore trials, and professional sprinklings I have been heir to, in the wild state that I have been living in for some length of time. I spent a very pleasant and profitable winter in the city, had many ups and downs, became quite learned, felt thankful to the professors for their many kind words of instruction, and thus ended my first course of lectures.

You see I have had to pass over many things that occurred during the winter. I attended the lectures closely, and made as many improvements, I venture to say, as any student in college. The last bell being rung by the janitor for the coming together of medical students, the last lecture delivered, the farewell of each professor pronounced, I took my last look of the dear old building, in which I had been advanced in the healing art. Though I was glad to return to the place of my boyhood and youth, though my heart was thrilled with tender emotions when I thought of meeting my aged mother again, and though I had often been wearied by the close attendance daily for several months, still I could not help shedding a tear when I left the old college. I thought my future success in life depended on the knowledge and instruction I had gained while I had been an inmate of its walls; it was to be my sheet-anchor in time of trouble, my standard for reference when sore trials should await me; but farewell! old halls of science, farewell! I now must stand on my own merits; no longer under thy protection. I went on board a steamer, and soon was wending my way down the beautiful stream, and in a few days was safe at that same old dwelling. I found that a few short months had wrought many important changes. Many of my lady acquaintances had changed their place of residence as well as their names. Many of my old friends had left the stage of action, and, still worse than all these changes, my preceptor had changed in his feelings toward me, or he had always been deceiving me. Previous to my departure to attend the lectures, he had told me that on my return he would take me in as a partner in practice. After visiting many of my relatives and friends, and enjoying myself in their society, I went to see my old preceptor, to have a talk with him about the future prospects of practice. Great was my disappointment to hear him say nothing about it. I began to fear that something was wrong, and was determined to know what it was, or have one of the biggest rows that I had ever been in yet.[1] After waiting a short time to see if he would not name the thing, I threw off all scruples about nice feelings, and named it myself. Says I "Doctor, I have been absent for several months endeavoring to prepare myself for practice; what have you to say about your proposal last fall?"

"Well—well—I—I—oh—there is not much practice doing; I don't much think there is enough doing to support us both. I would like it very well if I thought you could do well by it, but—but don't think you can. I think some place where the profession is not crowded would be better for a young physician commencing practice. If I was you I would—"

"You go to the wall with your wood and advice too, and I will go to the backwoods of Arkansaw, or some other hot climate."[2]

And so saying, I picked up my hat and toddled out, and that was the last I ever saw of him. I have managed to make a living without his help, from that time to the present. He gave no reason for his change of mind more than I have stated, but before I left the neighborhood I found out the reason why the old fellow changed his notion: he had another young man a student in his office, that was in better circumstances than I was, as regards property, but no better as to principle; for though I am a practitioner of medicine in the part of our great country that is yet almost uncivilized when compared with other portions, although this seclusion may be my lot for life, and though this little vol-

ume may be all the name I shall leave to posterity, I flatter myself
that a warmer heart never beat in human breast than mine. Yes,
my dear reader, I am now far from the scenes that then surrounded me; the place of my youthful associations is now lost to
sight, perhaps never again to be seen by me, and I am in a land of
strangers, where no kindred spirits can commune with mine.[3] I
have never beheld a face since I have been here that I laid eyes on
before; but yet I think I have warm hearts here that feel for me;
they appreciate my services, and look on me as a friend when
scorched with fever, or racked with pain. They shall not be deceived. I am with you still, to help when overtaken by the hand of
affliction; in me you shall find all that you have found up to the
present moment, and I feel that you will not forsake me when the
vile slanderer assails me in my absence. Well, it is useless to
think anything more about it now; it's past and can't be recalled,
and I would not recall the moments if I could. I am happy and
contented in my present situation in life, though humble it may
be, and that is more than many can say that are in better circumstances, and reveling in the crowded city. I returned from my old
preceptor, to my parental roof, and told my relatives of the
change in my prospects, and remarked to them at the same time
that a few more days and I must leave them, perhaps never to
meet them again.

Ah! reader, have you ever parted with relatives and friends,
with the expectation that you should never meet them again?
have you taken the affectionate mother by the hand and said to
her, Farewell! mother, I may never see you again; I must leave
you to seek my destiny in another land. If you have passed
through such a scene, you can form some idea of my feelings at
that moment. It was hard to leave them, but it could not be
helped. In a few short days I was ready to go, I did not know
where but go I must, to try my luck on my own responsibility. I
told my relatives I did not know where I should stop. I had as fine
a horse for the trip as ever kicked, and now, everything being

ready, I took the parting hand once more. It seemed to me, that I was never again to behold one of those that were so near and dear to me. It has thus far proved true; I have never seen one of them since. Some I never can see again, as they have long since passed from time to eternity. But now to my journey.

I started once more on the lonesome road. I traveled day after day until I arrived on the bank of the Mississippi river, in the southwestern part of Tennessee. Here I stopped for a day or two, studying whether to go to Mississippi or Arkansas. After thinking over the matter in every possible way, I concluded to go through Mississippi, and if I did not find a situation to suit me I would go on to Arkansas. I started early one morning and traveled until near night without stopping to rest more than a few moments at a time. I made good headway that day, but my horse, poor animal, was near tired down, as well as myself. I stopped at a house and asked if I could stay all night. The gentleman told me that I could. I got down, went in, and very soon found that I was perfectly at home. The old gentleman was very loquacious, communicative, and inquisitive. After supper I proposed to him that we go and see after my horse. He readily agreed. We went out, and, after seeing my horse, he remarked what a fine animal he was. "Yes, my occupation in life requires a horse that can stand the rubs."

"Pray, sir, what is that occupation, if I may be so inquisitive?"

"Certainly, sir, I like to see a man take interest enough in me to ask questions when he feels like it; I am a physician."

"Ah! indeed, you do require a good horse for that, if you intend to practice in the South. You will find many bad roads, bayous, bushes, and everything calculated to wear out man and horse. Where do you think of going to—some place in view I s'pose?"

"No, sir, God only knows where I will get to; I do not know a place on earth where I can find a practice; wish that I did. I have been studying a long time, spent most of my means, and I am *just now from College.* I have seen some practice, and think I could do well if I had any chance. Very discouraging, my friend, to a young man in my situation."

My history seemed to awaken some feelings of sympathy in the old gentleman, and he said to me:

"My young friend, I think I can tell you of a situation where you can do well; your friendly and kind disposition will secure you the good feelings of any community in which you may locate; I don't know whether you would like it or not; your practice would be a laborious one; you will be deprived of such refinements in society as you have, no doubt, been used to."

"It matters not, sir, about the labor or the refinements; anything for a year or two, until I get a start."

"Well sir, it is on Raccoon Bayou, Arkansaw; I have a friend living there, that writes me they need a doctor very much in his neighborhood; there is none nearer than twenty miles, and he hasn't sense enough to get out of a shower of rain in dry weather.[4] Come, let's go up to the house; I'll read you the letter."

We went in, he got the letter and read it, and it was as flattering as he had represented, as you will see by its perusal. I have the letter now in my possession: the old gentleman handed it to me that night, and I never returned it, as I wanted to show the writer of it that I had documents to show that a doctor could be sustained in his neighborhood. Here is the letter:

Racune Bio Arkunsau, Ap'l 3rd.

"Deer Sur:

"I taak and uppertuite to ryte yue ain. I hav bin mity sik cence you hurd from mee las. I hav bin grately infortunite indeed. I hav had thee Agger an feevor fur threa weaks,[5] I am sum bettur now seence I yousid thee doog-would biiters. I dount no whatt we will do ian ower cection iff a doktur dount seetel heare. We hav nun neerear then tad-pole slue an thatt are twenty myle. Sallye gott hur legg broak thee uther daa an eye seent fur doktur Cadely. Thee legg wass soe badd wheen hee goot

tu hur he sayed itt mus bee saud off. He comenced wythe hiss insur-
ments an bi jolley the fus thing eye nowed hee hadd oft thee legg an
thee rong *one* att thatt. Wheen hee had it drest eye lucked at itt an eye
were so madd eye coomenced on hymn and beat himn intu flynders.
Thee legg which were broked gott wel without anny trubble. Now iff
yue coud send us a doktur inn our naburhud weed bee mouch ablige,
wee kan giv hymn plenty off practyc, he shall not suffur if he will stay
heare—eye looke fur a leetur from you inn dew time, and hoap yue will
senn uss a doktur, our luv an komplimets to *awl,*

"Youer frend and wel wishur &c.,

JOHN HANLY."[6]

You may believe that I am exaggerating; but if any man doubts
it and will call on me, I will show him the original letter in
Mr. Hanly's own handwriting. I must confess that a letter written
in the style it was, did not seem very inviting, but this was all the
place that had been offered me. The old gentleman remarked that
Mr. Hanly was a bad scholar, but a better hearted man never
lived, and what he said could be depended on. He said that none
but "Quacks" had ever been in that part of the State, and if I was
from college I would do all the practice in the country. Let me
say, while I think of it, that as regarded Sally's leg being cut off
(the wrong one at that), was all a piece of fun of Mr. Hanly's; the
other part of the letter was true. We talked about the matter until
bedtime, and when I was going to bed, the old man told me to
sleep on it until morning. I retired, and though greatly exhausted
by my hard day's ride, I could not sleep for some time. I got up
next morning and told the old gentleman if he would give me an
introductory letter to his friend, I would go and see the situation.
He did so, and still further as a proof of his interest in my welfare,
he would not charge me anything for staying all night. He gave
me directions how to go, and I shuddered almost as he was doing
so, for I would have to go through the Mississippi bottom, cross
the river, and then encounter other things equally as desirable on

the Arkansaw side. I thanked the old gentleman a thousand times for his kindness, bade him good morning, and started on my journey.

I had three or four days more traveling before reaching my intended location. I arrived at the edge of the Mississippi bottom about 12 o'clock on the first day after leaving my old friend. Never have I had such feelings about what I would now call a small affair. When I arrived at the edge of the bluff, my horse looked down on the valley below as if he feared to venture in; I did not feel much better. I got down, stripped my horse, and rested myself for awhile. The road that led through the swamps was nothing but a path, or, I suppose persons accustomed to traveling in *the bottom*[7] would call it a wagon road. Persons were in the habit of driving vehicles of different kinds along the road when the water was low in the river in the summer season. They had not however, commenced yet, as the water was not dried up in the bayous, sloughs, &c., sufficiently to justify them in going through. I feared that I should lose my way, and then I knew I was a gone sucker.[8] But the task was before me, and I must decide. I was the first, I supposed, that had attempted to go through that spring. Well, I could never stand the thought of turning back; other persons had once gone through, why should I falter? I got ready and turned my horse down the way the path seemed to go; he went a few steps and stopped, then looked round at me, as much as to say, I don't want to go. Poor horse, I could not blame you; it was a dismal sight. Seeing that I would not accept of any apology from him, he went on. In a few minutes I was buried in the depths of a dense forest, bushes, briers, canes, thorns, sloughs, lagoons, and cypress knees. I looked round to see the bluff once more; 'twas lost to view, I couldn't see twenty steps. I had no other way now to look but onward; I knew that I did not have more than time to reach the first house by night; if I was left in the woods to spend the night, I was surrounded by bears, wolves, wildcats, panthers, snakes, and everything else that could destroy both man and horse. I went as fast as the condition of the road would permit, which was not very fast. I had been in the bottom for two or three hours, and considered that I was getting on finely, when a shock passed through my system by the sound of distant thunder. In a moment I recollected all the accounts I had read of tornadoes in the Mississippi valley; the tornado at Natchez, at Granada, and other places; they in all their horrid colors were at once before me. I still traveled on, as turning back would be as bad as going on. Louder and louder the thunder; nearer and nearer the clouds approached, and brighter still the lightning's flash. I found I had better get under the branches of the largest tree I could find; I looked around and saw a large oak: I rode out to it, got down, stripped my horse, laid down my saddle-bags, and covered them with my saddle to keep them dry. I had a large blue blanket with a hole cut in the middle, and an umbrella. Having put on the blanket and spread the umbrella, I was prepared to weather the approaching storm as well as circumstances would admit.

The sky is darkened, the angry cloud is lowering o'er me, and it breaks with a deluge of water. I could tell from the way my horse acted that it was going to be a dreadful gale. The poor creature, as if looking to me for help, stooped his head, put it under the umbrella, near my side, trembled, moaned, and looked anxiously at me. In a few moments his worst fears were realized, and let me say here for the benefit of those of my readers that are not already aware of the fact, that when you are traveling on horseback and a storm rises, you may tell from the actions of your horse if it is going to be a bad storm. Should he moan, tremble, and stand close to you, you may look out for a hard time.[9] It is perfectly useless for me, an old dried-up backwoodsman, to attempt a description of that storm: the rain fell in torrents, the trees were felled to the earth, and the ground on which I stood trembled like an earthquake was at hand. It continued unabated until nearly dark. Oh, horrible thought! in the middle of the Mississippi bottom; not a house or place of security nearer than ten miles; overtaken by night without anything for myself or horse to eat, and at the mercy of the wild beasts of this dark and benighted wood. It was very evident I could not get to any house that night: for even if the road was such that I could find it without any trouble, I would run the risk of being eat up by some wild animal. I concluded I had as well take lodgings for the night near the large oak. I found a place to put my saddle and saddle-bags, in a bending tree nearby. I tied my horse where he could eat green cane and bushes, and now for a place for my own carcass. I had with me a large knife and revolver; these afforded me a little protection. I looked for a tree that I could get into; and after look-ing a short time, I found one with a large fork. I managed to get into it, having previously put my blanket up by means of a pole. Notwithstanding my situation was not the most desirable, I felt thankful that I had been so fortunate as to get where I was.

Well, here I am, and won't it be the longest night that ever en-veloped human nature in darkness. It was just the commencement of musquito time,[10] and I did not have any cause for grumbling for the want of kin-folks: they all called me *Ku-Zene* (cousin), and though they were warned every few moments to *stick no bills*,[11] they pitched into me like pouring suds down a sink. Besides these friendly "gnawers," I had some others gnawing at me; for instance, a gnawing appetite, a gnawing conscience, and, worse than all these gnawings, three large hungry, gaunt-cutted, slab-sided, lopper-jawed, blackeyed, long-tailed wolves came up, gave a few loud howls, and commenced gnawing at the root of the tree in which I was located. Can it be that they can gnaw down a tree before morning? They had not been howling long until they raised as many more of their infamous tribe; and they all set up the most horrible noise that ever fell on my ear. The clouds had now cleared away, and it was a beautiful moonlight night. I felt bad enough with those wolves gnawing at the foundation of my security; but this was small compared with what my feelings were when I heard a loud piercing scream proceeding from what I thought were the lungs of a panther, and my diagnosis turned out right, for in a short time two or three of the largest, I suppose, that ever made a track in the Mississippi swamp made their appearance.[12]

Farewell to marble halls and two big frogs for supper—what a fix I am come to.

Was it possible, after all my misfortunes in life, my dangers, my escapes, that I must become food for wild beasts—my friends never to know where, when, or how I died. I was in a quandary what to do—I was thinking whether I would do something or do nothing, or not do something or nothing—in fact I thought the prognosis decidedly *grave.* The wolves and panthers set up a most terrible yelling and howling my horse broke loose and run off. This was making things no better fast, as I would be left in almost as bad a situation next morning, if I should live, without a horse, as I was then surrounded by such desirable friends, such good friends that they would eat my flesh if they could get it. In this truly unpleasant situation I passed the night, expecting every moment that the panthers would climb after me. If ever I was glad to see the dawn of morning it was then. I had been looking forward to that time with the hope that the wolves and panthers would leave me; that my nurses that had watched *under me* through the night would now seek some rest for themselves; but not so, they said; though they were tired and wanted sleep, they were unwilling to leave me while my situation was so dangerous. It seemed ungrateful to wound their feelings, after setting up with me all night, but I was compelled to do so to get some ease myself—not such an easy thing to sit all night in the fork of a tree. I was only fifteen or twenty feet from the ground, and when it was light enough I concluded to treat them to something for their trouble. I drew a bead on an old wolf, and let him have it just behind the left foreleg; he gave one short breath, and it was the last act of his life. This unexpected news alarmed the whole

I drew a bead on an old wolf, and let him have it just behind the left foreleg; he gave one short breath, and it was the last act of his life.

crowd, and off they all started like a cannonading had been let loose on them. This was the last of them, and I felt greatly relieved, as you may imagine, to get on the earth once more.

The first thing after I got down was to see to my saddle and saddle-bags, and to look for my horse. I found all things right except my horse. Now what was I to do? I could not wag out all my traveling utensils; did not know whether I could get out myself or not. I commenced looking round and calling him, and, true to his master, my good animal came out from a thick patch of bushes and cane where he had been secreted eating. I felt like doing something then, *I did.* I soon had all things ready again, and after that found but little difficulty in getting through the bottom, except occasionally a bayou to swim. In three days more I arrived at Raccoon Bayou, Arkansas, safe and sound. I delivered my introductory letter to Mr. Hanly, and though a poor scholar as regards spelling, he was very kind and gentlemanly in his deportment. He told me he thought his neighborhood was a fine location for a young man as I was, said he would do all he could for me, and that he had a great influence; knew every man in twenty miles square, and would board me and my horse for nothing, only if any of his family got sick I must cure them—the country was thinly settled, people scarce, and none to spare. Seeing that I had went so far, and being about out of the needful, I finally agreed to stay; and now commences a little of something else, as I have come to the incidents of my life that have occurred while I was an "Arkansaw Doctor."

CHAPTER XIII

MAKING A HOLE
IN THE WRONG PLACE

Air—Cornstalk fiddle and de shoe-string bow.

If you will listen, I'll relate
A truth that's worth your reading:
A negro in haste came to my gate
Saying, a doctor now is needin'.
I quickly went to see the case,
And thought I'd make a quarter:
How dear it was my time to waste,
In drawing off the water.

BOOT-BLACKER.

AFTER much difficulty I managed to procure me a supply of medicines for my office, and everything being prepared, I was ready to commence "pilling it." I felt the weight of responsibility: I was situated where I could not have the advantage of consultation in a tight place. I knew but little about the healing art, compared with my older brothers in the profession, and was yet young and knew but little of the usages of the sick room; but consoled myself in this respect, by thinking there were no usages in them parts only rough usage. Notwithstanding all this, I was determined to do the best I could, and that was all any man could do, and rest assured that I will give a plain and comprehensive description of cases as they occurred; not picking the cases that might suit my own taste; that is, not telling you of cases I cured, and leaving those that did not do well for my own reflection, the good and bad luck will all alike come before you. I am not going to give an account of every case I had. Far from it; that would require a large volume. I will give those of the most importance, the lucky and the unlucky. Mr. Hanly took the trouble to go around with me and make me known to the neighbors. Everybody seemed glad to think that I had come into the country to practice; they said I might depend on their support, let who come that might. I had been settled but a few days until I was put to the test of what I knew about medicine. I was sitting one afternoon in my office reading some medical book, when I was interrupted by the sound of horses' hoofs. I looked down the road and saw a negro on a horse, coming with all speed up to the office. In a few moments he was at the gate, and bawled out to know if there was a doctor living at that place. There was no other gentleman at the house but myself, and I stepped out and told him I was the doctor, and asked him what he wanted. Says he,

"Massa wants you to come as quick as you can to see a sick nigga at our house."

I asked him if the negro was much sick.

"Oh yes, massa, him's mitey bad."

I was soon ready, and away I went on my first visit in Arkansaw. We had ten miles to ride before reaching the patient. The old negro seemed to be very much alarmed about getting back with the doctor in time, and rode on more than a hundred yards ahead of me all the time. I found it useless to try to catch him, for every time that I would ride faster to overtake him, he spurred the tighter, and kept the same distance ahead. At such a rate we were not long in reaching the place of action. I got down, took off my saddle-bags, threw them across my arm very learnedly and went in. I found the gentleman that the negro belonged to sitting near his side, waiting anxiously for my arrival. When I entered the door he said to me,

"Good evening; I s'pose you are the doctor, from the appearance of—"

"Yes, sir, Doctor Rattlehead, at your service."

He did not wait long to talk about me, for he felt more interested about his sick negro—several hundred dollars gone if he died. He pointed the patient out to me, and related his symptoms in detail. I examined him minutely for a long time, drew a long breath, sweated freely, and found it hard to satisfy myself of the nature of his disease. I thought of every lecture I had ever heard, every page I could read, and could make it out nothing but a case of dropsy of the abdominal cavity. The negro was very much swollen and suffering great pain: he was rolling and tumbling equal to a printing press, groaning like a dead dog on a wood-pile, and sweating faster than "Doctor Thompson in a steam tub."[1] It was as plain as the nose on "Bradbury's" face,[2] that something had to be done soon, or there would be a dead negro, as certain as tearing your shirt.[3] I studied awful hard, looked very grave, and said but little. The old man began to look straight at my countenance, as much as to say what are you going to do? I bristled up courage enough to commence a conversation with him about the case. I told him I was sorry to say so, but that his negro was in a bad fix; for, said I, there is an effusion of serum in his abdomen. Not knowing what I meant by such terms, he asked me to explain myself. I did so, by telling him the negro had the dropsy of the belly, and that the water must be let off. He said that he did not think he had been sick long enough to have dropsy.

"It is doubtless, sir, quite an acute attack, and sometimes fluid will be thrown out rapidly."

We talked about the case for some little time, but he eventually said it was in my hands to do with as I thought best. I explained to him what was necessary to be done, and took the precaution to say, that sometimes it was the case, that a physician would tap a patient, and from some cause the water would not flow out; such might be the case with the negro, I could not tell; I would do the best, though, that could be done. I went to my saddle-bags, took out my instruments, and soon had things in readiness for making a hole in the negro's dinner box.[4] The negro was in so much pain that he did not notice whether I was going to *spike* him or put on a poultice. I made him get in a suitable position, and then for a sharp job, a hard job, a slick job, and in fact, one of the most jobbiest pieces of jobs that ever I jobbed at in all my natural life.[5] I had a pan ready to receive the water that should flow out. I felt most consequently squeamish in the region of my stomach and lungs, but actuated from pure motives—winning a great name, and the old man's good feelings, I thought it would not do to shrink from duty; I therefore, with all the solemnity of taking a chicken from roost at midnight, proceeded to perform the operation. I took up the trocar[6] and plunged it in, then withdrawing and leaving the canula[7] through which the water was to flow. The operation thus far was completed. I waited some little time for the "moving of the waters," but found it was no go; it turned out to be a *dry dropsy*.[8]

Now for another scrape. Is it possible that I am to lose my first case? If I do, the jig is up with me in these parts.[9] I withdrew the instrument, and told the old man that it turned out very much as I had told him. He did not seem to think I had done anything wrong. I also told him that as the external operation had failed, I would try internal remedies. I applied a strip of adhesive plaster over the wound, and made preparations for trying some other remedies. I concluded I had better try the effect of an emetic, to see if the negro had not been eating something that caused this enlarged condition of his old bacon and corn-bread reservoir.

(Why was it I had not thought of it before?) I mixed up a good dose of ipecac,[10] and gave it to him. I also made him drink freely of warm water while the old man was out pacing the yard, wringing his hands and crying, cause he thought his negro was going to die. In fifteen or twenty minutes he commenced trembling like a horse with the blind-staggers,[11] his eyes rolled up the white side, water commenced running from his mouth in strings as long as plough lines; he doubled himself up like he had the colic, and a-wh-ah-hic, he went at it in good earnest. I scarcely know what to compare the scene of the contents of his stomach to, but I think it looked a little more like the breaking up of the fountains of the great deep, than anything I ever saw. As regards the ejected material, it would rank well with the cleaning up of a horse-trough, the malt vat of a still-house, or a hog-pen on a washing day. He kept up his heaving and setting until he threw off near half a bushel. On examination it turned out to be green corn. After the negro got his breath a little, he was asked why he had done so, and was threatened with a good thrashing on his recovery, unless he told how many ears of corn he had eaten.

"Wy massa, me only cum fum de corn fele wid *twenty-two years of roasin corn*, and me eat um for dinner."

The negro was now out of danger, but I considered myself in danger, unless I could give the old man good reasons for tapping the negro. I told him that the corn had produced a rapid accumulation of fluid in the bowels, as he could see by the amount thrown off (and thrown in too I think), and as the negro would tell nothing of it, any man would have been under the same impression that I was. I explained to him how it was that the fluid was *in* the bowels instead of being *on* them, as in ordinary dropsy. I proved successful in curing the negro, and also in winning the old man's friendship and esteem as is proved by the continuation of his patronage. I fixed up and put out home, well pleased that I had escaped as well as I did.

CHAPTER XIV

A FISHING PARTY,
A GHOST, AND SUICIDE

Air—Sugar in de gourd and de way to get it out.[1]

> *Away to the beautiful lake, away,*
> *To catch the silver fish.*
> *Hush! what happened while we stay!*
> *More than anyone could wish.*
> *In despair he seeks relief*
> *By destroying his life—*
> *Let it be a ghost or beef,*
> *I know it's not my wife.*

DADDY LONGLEGS.

I ARRIVED at home after my first visit, at ten o'clock at night! I rested well during the night, and next morning Mr. Hanly had to ask me many questions about my success. I of course gave a glowing account of my operation, and after it failed, then restoring the patient by other means. He congratulated me on my good start, and said he had no doubt but that I would soon have practice enough. While we were talking, one of Mr. Hanly's daugh-

ters came out, and commenced talking of a fishing party that was
to come off the next day, and asked me if I would not like to go. I
remarked that I should be most happy to do so. She named over
the ladies and gentlemen that were going, and among others a
young man that I had often seen during my short stay there. I
thought from appearances he was a little in love with Miss Hanly.
Early next morning the party had all assembled. We put off in
fine spirits to a little lake five miles distant, that was celebrated as
a great fishing place. I asked the pleasure of accompanying one
of the *gals*. She consented, and very soon we had arrived at the
place intended for our amusement. Having tied our horses, and
made a few other little arrangements necessary on such occasions, we commenced operations. We had good luck in getting a
fine lot of fish in a short time. We had been fishing for some time,
when it was proposed that we have something to eat. A few nice
fish were soon prepared, and we sat down to partake of them.
The young man that was so much in love with Miss Hanly, was
eating away at the rate of a fish a minute, and all at once he
dropped every thing and commenced looking most tarnal strange
for a man that had any sense. The tears streamed from his eyes in
drops as big as pears; his arms were raised to his head; his legs
stretched out and quivering like a dying calf; his head he was trying to put between his shoulders; he gasped as if in the last
agonies of death; a few faint struggles and he fell prostrate to the
earth. It can easily be imagined what was the matter; he had a fish
bone cross-*ways* in his red lane.[2] Everything was alarm and confusion, and in this state of excitement, I rushed to his side and had
his mouth open to see if I could reach the bone. I saw it, but so
far down that I could not extract it with my fingers. I ran to my
saddle-bags as quick as possible, knowing that time was precious. I returned as soon as I could get out my instruments, but
saw a great change in that short time. He was lying pale, relaxed,
and senseless. I took a pair of forceps, introduced them, and soon

had the bone out; but it seemed that he was too far gone to recover, several minutes having elapsed since the bone was lodged
in his throat. I made use of the usual means for restoring animation, such as throwing water in his face, hartshorn to his nose,
rubbing his chest, and rolling him about. Finding all these mea-
sures had failed, I tried, as a last resort, rolling up his trousers,
taking some half dozen large switches, and laying it on him with
all my power. This acted finally, and soon he was restored to
consciousness. He appeared thankful that I had saved his life, but
did not like the thought of getting a frailing for it.

In a short time all things were going on as well as ever, and it
was named that we all fish a little more before starting home. The
young man just rescued from his perilous situation was as lively
as if nothing had happened. His name I had as well tell you, as he
has moved off from those parts long since. His name was Bill
Dods, a short way of expressing ourselves in this country; everybody goes by the name of Jack, Tom, Dick, Sal, and Jake. Some
of the young men happened to bring along a little old whisky,
and after dining they got to feeling as big as elephants; and I believe Bill Dods was a little larger than anyone else; he did not
quit his fishing, though, until in one of his tantrums he jerked his
hook a little the wrong way and stuck it through Miss Hanly's
nose, tearing it at a great rate. Poor girl! she screamed like a panther, bled like a butchered hog for a few moments, fainted, and
fell to the ground. Again my services were needed. She was soon
resuscitated, and then came a little of her father's spunk. As soon
as I had dressed the wound she turned round to Bill Dods and
gave him instructions never again to come into her presence, or
dare to speak to her. Bill, poor fellow, looked like he was thun-
derstruck. He was so bad hurt at the language of Miss Hanly, that
he was perfectly speechless. In this condition of things we broke
off and went home, leaving Bill to go his own way.

When I reached home there was a summons waiting for me to

attend a patient some five miles up the bayou. It was now half past two in the afternoon. I started, thinking I was getting into practice fast. I found the patient suffering with common chills and fever, prepared the necessary medicine, and, after staying a short time, to make some *good impressions,* I left for home. I had proceeded a mile or two when my attention was attracted by the strange actions of my horse. He was more frightened than ever I had seen him, and I knew it must be something unusual that would cause him to be frightened so bad. I was fearful that a panther or some wild beast was near. I looked around to see what was the cause of all this. I saw something suspended in the air, two or three hundred yards ahead of me; the strangest looking specimen of creation that I ever laid eyes on. It was working and twisting about like a pig in hot slop,[3] a goose with his head in a crack, or a medical student out of money at a boarding-house several hundred miles from home. I got off of my horse, took my saddle-bags on my arm, and concluded to lead my horse up to the spot and see what it was. This I should not have done, had it not been that it had the appearance of some human being in distress. My horse was unwilling to go for a moment, but I went up to him, patted him on the head, and gave him to understand all was right, and he followed me without any trouble. Strange to say, that horse was so constituted that when I patted him in that way he would follow me anywhere I might go. I went up, and there I saw a young man, seemingly in the last agonies of dissolving nature; which, on examining a note that I found lying on the ground, turned out to be Bill Dods, who had committed suicide. He had went up the tree, from appearances, with a rope to commit the deed, by tying the rope round a large limb that made out from the trunk fifteen or twenty feet from the ground. How it was that he happened to hang himself by the middle instead of one end, I was left to make what inference I might. The rope was tied fast round his neck with one end, while the other was hanging loose. I came to the conclusion, that he had been sitting on the limb fixing the rope round his neck, or, perhaps, studying whether to hang himself or not, and accidentally lost his balance, and in doing so the fundamental portion of his trousers had caught over a small snag that made out from the limb. I was standing there making my calculations about these things, when I saw him move again, as though he was making his last feeble effort to save his life. He was evidently nearly dead, and how to save him I did not know. I was a poor climber, and it was a bad tree, a little snurly oak.[4] I thought it would never do to let the fellow die, without trying to save him. Such an ignominious death would break the hearts of his parents. I tied my horse, went up to the tree and commenced ascending; I made poor progress, but reached the limb after a powerful exertion. Under almost any other circumstances I could not have accomplished it. I cautiously went out on the limb, and, after reaching him, I found I could not extricate him by lifting. I saw no other alternative but to take my big knife and cut out a yard square from his *tow breeches*.[5] This I did, and down he went like a lump of dirt, to the ground. I hurried down, and found the vital spark was not entirely extinct. I out with my lancet, quick as thought, and bled him freely from the arm. I did this because his head had been hanging down, and there was certainly great engorgement of the brain, and perhaps effusion of blood. It was all the remedy that presented any prospect of relief. He very soon showed symptoms of returning life, and before half an hour, was sitting up tolerably comfortably, considering the blood he had lost, and his previous dilemma. I did not say anything to him about the note or the intended suicide, but managed to get him upon my horse and carried him to his father's, a mile or two from where I had found him. His parents were much surprised to hear of such an occurrence. After taking supper with them, I bid them goodnight, and was in the act of leaving, when I was told Bill wanted to see me. I went into the room where he was, and he told me for God's sake to keep the matter a secret, or he was a ruined man. He thanked me for this second time saving his life. I then went on home. I had the note in my pocket that I had picked up under the tree where Bill was hanging, and whether to destroy it or not I did not know. I thought there could be no harm in keeping it, and did so. When I got home I could not keep from having a little fun with Julia Hanly. I thought if Bill did not like it, he might go to the left mid-ter-sheep, or Jericho,[6] I did not care which; I had saved his life twice, and he had never offered me anything but "thanks" for it, and that didn't pay.

As soon as I got in the house I called for Julia and handed her the letter from Bill, who thought he would be in eternity when that was read by the fair one. She made some little to do, but not so much as I thought she would. She showed it to her father and all the family. The old man said, if Bill wanted to take a pleasure trip to the devil, let him go, but that would not cure Julia's nose. Here I consoled him by saying that I would cure it without a scar if any man could do it. I then had to tell all the joke, and of all the laughing that I ever heard toll out of human natur', the old man beat it. If I had known it, I had just as well stuck up an advertisement on every tree in those woods about the matter, as to tell old man Hanly. Very soon it was known for twenty miles square. Bill knew it was me that had let the affair leak out, and he got awful mad at me. A few days after this, being called to see the same patient who had relapsed, if I recollect right, by some carelessness, I was returning home about nine o'clock that night, and got near a place that was said to be *haunted;* scarcely any person in the neighborhood would pass that place at night alone. Such was the superstition that even the Indians, that still lurked about in the forest twenty or thirty miles off, were unwilling to see the place at night.[7] I was coming near the place, and I thought of what dreadful tales I had heard of the ghost. When I got within a few rods of the spot all at once my horse became dreadfully frightened at a ghost, or whatever it was, and would not move a peg.[8] The sight before me was truly a fearful thing to think of. It looked like an angel; it had large wings, which were extended as if in the act of taking flight to the regions above; it was white as snow;[9] some strange ornament on the head, and in short, it looked *prodigious*[10] to a man in the forest, surrounded by wild beasts, two or three miles from any house or human being. On each side of me was a dense forest through which I could not go. There was but one way to get home, and that was the narrow road, in the middle of which stood this hideous ghost, or what you may call it. I could not think of turning back to the house of the patient where I had just left. I was determined to try something else to make the beautiful creature give me the road for a moment. I again patted my horse, and laid my arms around his neck. I knew then he would go or die; for he wanted his supper as bad as I wanted to get past that place. I took the law on my shoulder, and said, "Who's there?" No one spoke, and then I reined up my horse steadily and gave him the word. He got within about twenty steps and stopped. I had nothing but star-light to see by, but thought I could hit as large an object as the one before me. I raised up, fired away, and you had better think I did too, for if ever you heard yelling, bawling, throwing off of white things, rolling, ranting, cursing, and gubbing it up,[11] you could have heard it on that occasion. A man in ghost's clothing, and he was felled like a tree in new ground. I went up and there saw Bill Dods, with a big bullet passed through his left shoulder, as a remuneration for his attempt to sprinkle me with ghost feathers.

Notwithstanding I was not pleased with his treatment toward me after saving his life on two occasions, I took him upon my horse to his father's. The young man was too badly wounded for his parents to say anything to him at that time. I explained to them how it happened. They justified me in so doing, and asked if I would not dress the wound, and also attend him until it was well.

After fixing Bill up comfortable, I went home. I attended him until he got well, which was not very long, and made out a bill against his father for thirty dollars; he paid it, and Bill left for parts unknown, and has not been heard of since.

CHAPTER XV

TAKEN CAPTIVE
BY INDIANS

Air—Will thou give thy scalp?

Through the dark and shady wood
For nine long hours we toiled—
Little needen, little done,
I must return by light of sun;
No comfort for you, stranger, here—
Then good-bye—Oh! the red man now
Surrounds me, and I am lost:
Sleep on, no more you'll hear it thunder.

BRUTHER BEETLE-NOSE.

Now that Bill Dods was gone, my troubles with him were over. My practice gradually increased until I had as much as wanted to attend to in a country where there were scarcely any roads. It is true I had but few patients, compared with a physician in a thickly settled country, or a city practitioner, but they were so scattered that I was busy most of the time. I often went twenty-five and thirty miles. One morning while at breakfast, some person hollowed at the gate for me. I went out, and he told me he wanted me to go to see a sick woman some twenty-eight miles across the country. After we got our breakfast we started. We swam our horses across the bayou, and struck a little trail that led through the forest. It was in a different direction from any that I had ever been, and the road was entirely strange to me. I endeavored to notice as many of the peculiarities as possible, knowing I would have to return alone. After passing through many swamps, crossing bayous, cutting cane, and bogging a few times, we arrived safe at the house where the lady was sick. I soon found I had traveled a long ways for little purpose. The patient was an old lady that was of an industrious nature, and the day previous she had been making a big pot of soap which required her attention the whole day. Her husband coming home drunk about dark, had upset the pot, and away went all the woman's hard labor. Returning from the spring with a pail of water on her head, she saw the work of destruction, gave one loud, long keen "*O, me!*" and fell down with a fit of hysterics. This was the first attack she had ever had, and it soon sobered her husband to his senses. In this state of things he ran off for one of his neighbors. All their efforts proved unsuccessful in restoring her to consciousness, and there she lay, gulping and snuffing, without any prospect of relief. They had heard of my whereabouts, and fearing a fatal termination of the case, the old man succeeded in procuring the services of his friend as messenger for me. I found her pretty much as when the messenger started for me.

After resting a few moments, I proceeded to give her a good shower bath; that is, it was not exactly like your city shower baths, water running out of holes made in tin, but pouring a bucketfull or two slap-dash at once. This soon brought her to her *natural feelings*, and the first thing she said was—

"Tom, you scoundrel, what made you turn over my soap? Now you may wash your own clothes."

Tom promised to do better in future. This, with two big as-safetida pills, soon set all right.[1] I gave instructions to the old man how to act should she have another attack; then bidding them good-day, started home. There were but few houses on the way, and I had to travel well to reach the house of an acquaintance about half way between there and home. I thought I could get there by dark. I had gone four or five miles, when I was over-taken by a rain and considerable storm. I sheltered myself under a large bending tree the best I could, and, after the rain was over, started on my way again. I saw it was getting late, six o'clock or later. I made but slow progress, owing to the canes, vines, bushes, &c., being blown across the path. I went on until dark, and as it was yet five miles to the house of my acquaintance, I concluded I had better stop at a little cabin on the roadside, just ahead of me. I rode up to the house and hallooed. A little boy out in the woods heard me and came up, when the following dia-logue took place.

Doctor.—"My little boy, what's your name? can I get to stay all night with you?"

Boy.—"Mr. my name is same as my daddy's; don't think you can stay all night here; we no way komidatin' strangers nohow."

Doctor.—"I am willing to put up with any sort of fare, so I can stay; can't you find some place for my horse, and feed him a little?"

Boy.—"*Well, I reckin not;* for we haint no stable, an' we haint no corn, nor we haint no *fodder neder.*"

Doctor.—"Well, if I tie my horse up, can't you find some place for me to sleep?"

Boy.—"*Well, I reckin not;* kaise we haint no bed, nor we haint no straw, nor we haint no *floor in de house nedur.*"

Doctor.—"That looks pretty bad, my boy; but if I stop, can't you give me something to eat? I feel hungry; had no dinner to-day."

Boy.—*"Well, I reckin not;* kaise we haint no meet, nur we haint no bred, nor we haint no *taiter nedur."*

Doctor.—"How do you all do about here, then?"

Boy.—"Ah, tolable,[2] thank ye, sir; how do you do yourself? Good-bye, sir—dad's gone out to steal some now."[3]

Doctor.—*Tooked wid a leavin.* Feeling somewhat insulted at such language from a little knock-kneed, bow-legged, bandy-shanked, dried-up, hump-backed boy, I rode off and left him in his glory and in his shirttail. I thought perhaps I could find the way, or at least my horse could. I suppose I was about two miles and a half from where I left the boy, and that was the nearest human habitation in any direction. I was going along thinking I would soon be at my friend's house. The clouds had cleared away a little, and the moon would alternately cast a light, and then a shadow over that silent and dismal wood. I was looking forward with sweet anticipation of the future, summing up in my mind how much I had made since my commencement; occasionally the thought that I was in a dreary wilderness, surrounded by ravenous beasts, would cast a damper over my feelings, but hoping soon to be— Hark! my horse suddenly stops, raises his head, and I feel his big heart beating convulsively under me. I hear a rustling in the bushes close to me: my hair is standing on end:[4] I look around me: I behold a faint light, and in a moment the mystery is revealed. I hear a sound that falls like the death knell upon my ear; it sends a terror to my heart; I know it is the red man of the forest; the enemy of pale faces, the heartless savages. I know too that I am at the mercy of those who heed not the cry of the infant on its mother's bosom, and regard not the gray hairs of age. Thousands on the frontiers have, in their turn, fallen a prey to the tomahawk and scalping knife; now it is for me to be shot down like a dog, or burnt at the stake amid the shouts of these ungodly beings. Scarcely had those thoughts passed through my mind before I heard the Indians set up a horrid yelling. My horse dashed off in a moment, and endeavored to make his escape; but alas! my noble animal, it was in vain, I was surrounded. One of the Indians jumped before my horse with hatchet in hand, and caught him by the bridle. I was quickly taken off, and found myself in the hands of six big Indians. They were in the act of ransacking my saddle-bags, but when they got the scent of the medicines they let them remain on my horse. They then put out the fire, and after talking (I could not tell what about) for a little while, they gave me signs to mount my horse again. Whether they did it because they were afraid to ride the horse or not I could not tell. One of them took my horse by the bridle and started off, the others all following after. *This is practicing medicine with a long pole.* Now I am in for my last scrape certain; no use thinking about anything else. I thought of my past life, my many mishaps, and thought how much better it would have been for me had I been carried from the stage of action in some past difficulty, when some trace of me could have been left; but now to be burnt at the stake—the most awful death! I remembered every narrative I had read of Indians, their manners and customs, their cruelty, their barbarous conduct.[5] I finally quietly resigned myself to the will of Him that holds the destiny of man: that if it was to be my lot I could not help it now; I had put myself in danger; I must abide the consequences. We traveled all that night, only stopping occasionally to rest. I took the precaution to observe the direction in which we went, so that if an opportunity should present to escape, I could tell in what direction home was. We went a northwest course. We traveled until eleven o'clock next day, when we arrived at the wigwam of the Indians. There was a considerable number at the place. They gave me signs to take off my saddle and tie my horse. I did so, and if ever I felt sorry for anything in my life, it was for my poor horse; he was so hungry and tired he could scarcely stand. I tied him where he could eat grass, bushes, and such things as he could get.

Ah! reader, you may imagine how I felt, but its more than I can now express; death viewed in any light, even when surrounded by a kind father, an affectionate mother, a dear sister, a good brother, or a devoted companion, is sad enough; but to think of dying by the hands of an Indian in the forest, far from friends or home, is painful beyond description. I went up to the wigwam of the Indians who had captured me;[6] they motioned me to come in, and offered me some venison to eat, which I could not refuse, for I had an appetite like a crosscut-saw,[7] having eat nothing for more than twenty-four hours. After eating, I looked for them to commence operations on me in some way, but in this I was happily disappointed. They did not trouble me or take much notice of me for several days, and let me go about and attend to my horse, holding him to eat grass, and watering him. They gave me plenty to eat, and also to drink of whisky, when they had it. I slept in the wigwam on my blanket, and my saddle-bags under my head for a pillow. I was at a loss to know what they intended to do with me, but one day thought I would soon find what was going to be done, for they got to quarreling while drinking whisky, which I found was about me, and one of them made at me with a hatchet, and would have killed me but for another Indian running before me, who caught the blow himself in the arm. It was a bad cut, and would have been worse had the force not been checked by his other hand. It commenced bleeding profusely, which put a stop to the fight. They did not do anything to stop the blood, only to apply some leaves to it.[8]

I thought this a favorable time to get their goodwill, and went to my saddle-bags, took out my things and motioned the Indian what I wanted. He sat down on the ground, and by means of tying a small artery or two, and using an astringent, I soon stopped the bleeding. I then brought the edges together with strips of adhesive plaster and in a few days his arm was well. This made a great impression, and they thought me a superior being. Notwithstanding this, I found it useless to think of getting away from them, unless I could find some means to take advantage of them. They were in the habit of going off during the day to hunt, and occasionally took me with them. They dressed me after their own savage manner, and seemed very proud of me.

Things went on in this way for three weeks. I was anxious to be at liberty, but saw no chance of escape until on one occasion, when they had some whisky, which they had obtained at Fort Smith or Van Buren. The distance to either of these places, from where the Indians had me I could not tell. They had a big spree while the whisky lasted, and next day all of them went out hunting except six or seven. In looking in the jug they found all the whisky was not out, as the other Indians had thought. They commenced on it, and were getting to be "Indian big man," very fast. They made me drink also, and I just saw what would become of me if the whisky held out long enough, and the other Indians did not come in. While they were making merry without, I slipped into the wigwam to see how much more whisky was left. There was enough to set them in a fine way for killing me, to pass off the time while they had nothing else to do more profitable or easier accomplished. Now or never was my time, I thought, no time was to be lost. I searched my saddle-bags, and found two oz. of laudanum and a vial of morphia; also, a vial of paregoric. To make sure work of it I put all of these into the whisky, put all things back again, and laid down like I was drunk or asleep. It was not long until they came in, and then was a trying moment. If they tried to wake me was I to remain still? if so, they might drive a tomahawk into my senses. If I waked up, they would make me drink with them, and then I would be in as bad a fix as they. They came to me and gave a few "uh-ha-wa-hos!" but I would not wake; I knew it would only be death anyhow, and was resolved on trying to make them think I was drunk. Should the other Indians come in after they had drank the whisky and before I got off, and they were to die, then I should be killed. I was successful in my attempt at feigned drunkenness, they let me alone, and drank the whisky themselves. I waited in awful suspense and the deepest anxiety for the opiate to stupefy them and permit me

to get off before the hunters came in. Thank heaven! I was not
long left in this situation until I heard them utter a few deep
groans, and then, falling into a deep, snoring coma, they were all
soon in the arms of sweet Morpheus.[9]

Now is the golden moment. I quickly had my saddle on my
horse, and, going back for my clothes and saddle-bags, I bowed
politely to them, mounted, and was soon lost to view in the deep
recesses of the thick woods. My horse seemed to know every
inch of the way, and carried me swiftly from my place of bond-
age. I traveled as fast as I could, not knowing what moment the
hunters might come in and start in pursuit of me. I had no fears of
the six drunken ones following me, for old opium, bless the article (in the right place), was fast wafting them to that wigwam
whence no Indian returns. That was my private opinion about
the matter, and though I did not yet feel safe, I could not but con-
gratulate them on their indulgence in a good long nap. My horse
seemed more happy to get away from the camp than I possibly
could be, and though he had been tied up for three weeks, he
traveled without in the least showing signs of fatigue. I went on
until dark without molestation. At this time my feelings were
anything but pleasant. I thought I was on the right direction
home, judging from the moss on the trees, this being my principal guide. And here let me say to those of my readers that are
not acquainted with backwoods life, that should they ever become
members of such a community, they will, in traveling through
the forest find this an infallible guide; the moss always growing
on the north side of the trees. I thought I had better rest a little,
and therefore got down, let my horse eat some grass, while I
helped myself to some dried venison I had brought with me from
the camp. After this my horse and myself were much refreshed. I
mounted again and resumed my travel, taking the precaution to
see that my pistol (which I had kept concealed during my stay
with the Indians) was well charged, and put my big knife so I

could lay hands on it at any moment, not knowing when I would be attacked by wild beasts or pursued by the Indians.

Happily for me the moon was shining for a short time in the early part of the night. I rode as fast as I could while the moon was shining, fearing I could not find my way after that luminary had ceased to light my path. I got along without much difficulty while I had moonlight, but after that I had many troubles. Occasionally, while going along, I could hear coons and bears, running up and down the trees, as though they were on a smooth sidewalk in a city; loud keen screams of the panther, the cries of wildcats and howl of wolves; but I proceeded unharmed until near midnight. I, as well as my horse, was almost exhausted from the long continued fatigue; I did not know whether I had kept the right direction or not, or when I should again behold a human face. I was desponding, and thought my lot a hard one, when, to my great joy, I heard in the distance the lonely sound of the cowbell. I knew I was near a settlement; I followed in the direction of the sound for near an hour, and just as the light of day was dawning I rode up to the house where the old lady that had the hysterics lived. By the time it was light I had aroused the inmates, and there was a happy set of folks for you. I found the cabin as full as it could hold of neighbors, who had been out several days on the hunt for me, and, not finding me, were on their return home.

It was on that occasion I felt that though in a land of strangers, far from every kindred tie that bound me to earth, I was not uncared for; that my worth was appreciated; that there were yet some warm hearts that beat for me. I had to relate my adventures while absent, and when I told them about knocking the susceptibilities out of a half dozen Indians with so little trouble, I never saw a set of men more highly pleased in all my life. We got breakfast, and went off home in fine spirits. I was so much engaged I could not call on my red brethren to see whether they lived or not but I have no doubt but they did well.

CHAPTER XVI

THE MAN WITH
A SNAKE DISEASE

Air—Our way across the swamp.

List, thou fiery serpent,
  And leave your resting place,
Long, long will you repent
  That you occupied such space.
Doctor, I've suffered this many year
  With—and—a—sort of wheezin';
Hush! Polly, nothing the matter but fear—
  Drot your melt, I'll give you a greasin'.

YALLER BRITCHES.

I WAS scarcely left at leisure long enough to rest, before I was sent for to see an old man, some ten miles down the bayou, who had been sick for a long time, and he was no better than when first taken. The messenger that came for me was a favorite old negro belonging to the man that was sick. When he came up I asked him who was sick; he said, "Ole massa." I asked him who his master was.

"Wy, wy, God bless you, sir, I thought ebery body know ole Massa: his name Tom Dupree."

I told the negro to wait a few moments, and I would be ready. I went in the office to get something—well, when I say office I mean it, but it was only a little log house used for an office, in common with several other things, such as shelling corn of wet days, putting the saddles in, getting drunk in when they wanted to, and many other things not worth naming. Well, as I was coming out of the door, Mr. Hanly hailed me:

"Hello, Doc! who's sick?"

"Mr. Dupree, the negro calls him."

"Ha, ha, ha, Doc, you had as well try to grin off a bear's tail at midnight, as to cure that old man; every old quack, Indian, and midwife in Arkansas has tried on him without doing any good; he imagines he has a snake in his insides, and unless you can get that away, you can't cure him, and you well know you can't do that, for there is no more snake in him than there is in you."[2]

"Well, it is my duty to try on every case that comes up, and I will go once and see him anyhow."

Mr. Hanly said that he would pay me as long as I held out any hope of curing him, for, said he, "A fortune or two has been spent on him already; he has confidence as long as a man tells him he can cure him."

We started, and I soon found the old negro was more loquacious than I wanted him to be, and therefore did not encourage him any. The first thing he spoke of was, that if I could cure his master he would give me *heap money,*[3] and that people down in his parts, said as how I was a great doctor.

When I got there I found the old gentleman with his hands crossed over his breast, flat on his back on the floor, and his wife with pipe in mouth, pouring poke juice down his throat.[4] This she stopped when I got in, and she and the old man commenced talking, and giving a history of the disease; this doctor and that doctor had tried him and all did him no good, made him worse and had it not been that I stopped them they would have been at it yet. They would not give me time to slip in a word edgeways for at least two hours. At the end of this time, finding I could stop them no other way, I took up my saddlebags and started out as if I was going home. They could not have been worse shocked if a buffalo had fallen through the house top horns foremost, than when I started out. They stopped for a moment, and I told them they must not tell me anything more about the sickness, or I could not cure it. The old man did think that he had a snake in his belly sure enough, and everyone that tried to cure him had laughed at the absurdity of the notion, and tried to persuade him out of it. It all did no good; he had the same notion still. I saw the foolishness of his notion, but thought I would try a different course from what had been done by others. I told them I was of the same opinion as they were, and thought he had a snake in his belly, and unless it was got out he would never get well. I never saw people cut as many capers[5] in my life, as they did, when they found a doctor of the same opinion as they were about the snake. The old man told the very night that the snake crawled down his throat, while he was asleep on the woodpile. I told him if he would give me fifty dollars I would cure him, and if I did not show him the snake before I was done, I would not charge him a cent. He agreed in a moment. I told him I would have to go into the woods, to find a certain herb that would kill the snake, and then I could get it up easy enough.

I started out and found some lobelia,[6] the very thing I wanted, the very one I needed, and I knew I could find it easy enough, and besides that, if I gave him any medicine out of my saddle-bags, he would think it was the same old tune; something new was to be tried to meet his freak of fancy sickness. After finding the lobelia, I returned and asked the old lady for a skillet to boil it in. She wanted to go into the kitchen with me to help about it; I told her no; that I was dealing with a snake, and must do every-thing myself. I put the lobelia on to boil a few moments, went out, got an old gourd, and went off to the woods again. I found a small black-snake without much trouble, managed to weary him down, put him in the gourd, filled it with water, and soon had him as dead as a mackerel.[7]

You must not think strange of me saying I found a snake so easy, for they are as plenty in Arkansaw as musquitoes or buffalo gnats.[8] I left the snake in the kitchen, went in to the old man, and told him he must have a handkerchief over his eyes, as he would not then be so sick, took out mine from my pocket and put it on, blindfolding him completely. I then asked the old woman to step out in the wood a little, as I wanted to be alone for awhile with the old man. I went for the snake and lobelia, and I gave him a rip-snorting dose of it, and it was not long in displaying its effects, for in a few minutes he commenced throwing up more bread, po-tatoes, pieces of deer meat, and turnip tops, than would make a dinner for the Bull-frog tavern at Pine Bluff.[9] While this was going on I put the snake into the vessel, threw away the gourd and lobelia, and in one of his greatest upturnings, I hallooed out at the top of my voice, "*hurraw* my old fellow, you will get well now." By the time I had said it, he had off the handkerchief and squalled out—

"Betsy, Betsy, Betsy! there it is at last!"

Betsy ran in, and then a thousand blessings were showered on my head, plenty of whisky down my throat, and *fifty dollars in my pocket.* The old negro came running up and said:—

"God bless de doctor fureber, ole massa got de right un at last."

I ordered a purgative of calomel, rhubarb, and aloes—a favor-ite purgative in the south and west, passing under the name of *Cook's Pills*—told the old man to be careful of his diet, never sleep on the wood-pile again, bathe twice a day for a week in cold water, and he would never know what sickness was anymore.

That was a great job for me, not only because I got fifty dol-lars, but everybody thought I was the best doctor on earth, and because—because—you'll find out before you get through reading this book. I never told anyone of the cheat until now, and you may consider yourself fortunate in getting it, as it is done at the risk of friend Tommy Dupree and Betsy hearing of it.

As I was returning home, I was called in to see a woman troubled with some complaint not of much importance, but I shall always recollect one thing that happened, and a day after, probably: here it is. The woman commenced telling me a great tale of her sickness; this was the matter, and that was not right, and I don't know what, until her husband said to her—

"*Polly,* I don't think you are much sick, making me pay a dollar for nothing."

Fire and blazes, how mad she got. She came out on him like a blue streak of lightning,[10] and kept up for some time. Finally he said to her if she didn't hush he would make her. She was too good pluck to bear such an insult as that, even from a distant relative, as her husband was: so she just raised herself up and fastened on to the first thing she could get, which happened to be a great long string of *sassingers*[11] stuffed in guts; and if she didn't give him one of the greatest drubbings that ever I saw then you can have my noggin for a spit-box. She didn't need any medicine.

CHAPTER XVII

CUTTING UP
A NEGRO ALIVE

Air—I dreamt I was in a nigger cabin.[1]

Bring your brandy, pour it down,
A warm bath will restore him;
Farewell, death's relieved his pain—
Now, doctor, please to carve him.
Good God! massa, Dick not dead,
And you are sawing on his head.
My side's in pain; his eye's not stout;
Murder! the pain is worse—his eye is out.

BILLY DISHRAG.

HAVING met with such unprecedented success in curing those that were put under my care, I was called for very often, and could not be had at any price. I had returned one day from a distance very much fatigued, and had laid down for a short repose. I had not been asleep long, until I was waked up to go in haste to see a negro belonging to a gentleman in the neighborhood. I was soon ready and went as fast as possible, as it was said the patient

I was sawing away on Dick's brain-holder, and him not dead.

was *very dangerous*. I found this to be the case on my arrival, for the negro was as stiff as a poker, as senseless as an iron wedge, and breathing with as much noise as a stern-wheel steamboat on a bar. His hard breathing, cold extremities, clammy perspiration, rigidity of the muscles, &c., I thought was a good indication of a congestive chill. I could make nothing else of it, and began treating it as such. The first thing I did was to get some stimulating fluid down his throat. I succeeded in getting a little brandy down him. I then had a large tub of warm water prepared, and put him into it. I wish you may stop my nose with red wafers and wheatbran, in a flower garden or a dissecting room, if he didn't keel right over like you had shot him. The fact is he never kicked after striking the water. I felt most gallinipperatious uncomfortable about it, but could not help it. I did it all for the best, in accordance too with what I had been taught. I told the bystanders that he was too far gone—very common expression with doctors, you know. The gentleman that the negro belonged to, sent word down from the "white folks' house" that he had not owned the negro long, and wanted me to examine him to see of what disease he died, as he might have a lawsuit about him.

I was glad of an opportunity of trying my instruments on his tough skin, and without much ceremony went at it. I thought I would commence on the head first, then the chest and abdomen. I sheared off the wool and made a circular incision around the head to the bone. Well, about this time I was troubled to know what I should do for a saw to get through the bone; I had none in my case. We finally found an old rusty saw that was lying in the loft, and with that I commenced sawing away. It reminded me of the old dissecting room at college, only one was in the backwoods of Arkansaw, the other was in a large and populous city: one was performed by a sort of a cobbler, the other by a wise old head and steady hand. I drew the saw across once or twice, when I saw something that made me feel about as desirable as sitting on a mill-stone in the gulf of Mexico. The negro's head moved without any assistance from me, and one old darkey bawled out:—

"Good God! massa, Dick not dead."

I was sawing away on Dick's brain-holder, and him not dead. Farewell, vain world, and pull my nose out; what now! He groaned a time or two and commenced vomiting; this soon started the circulation again, and in a short time the poor negro, with his head cut to the bone all round, was able to talk. I was puzzled no little to tell how I had been so much deceived. I had felt his pulse and everything that is usually done I had attended to, and all in the house thought him as dead as a hammer.[2] I thought, though, when I was cutting round his head that the blood run very free for a dead negro, but never imagined but what he was dead. I felt all over in spots as big as a blanket, but it was done now, and I must help myself to a piece of get out of the scrape. The owner had requested it, and therefore I did not feel as guilty as if I had proposed it myself. I set to work quick as I could, to repair the injury done. This I did by the usual means, such as bringing the edges together by sutures (stitches) and strips of adhesive plaster, and also a wash of sugar of lead and opium. After doing this I thought I would ask the negro a few questions and see what I could find out. I commenced in an abrupt manner as I was not pleased at the idea of losing such an opportunity of gaining information. The negro seemed alarmed immediately, and said—

"I won't do so no more; won't do so no more."

"Won't do what?" said I.

"Wy—wo—I—I—made a strong tea of *Bull Vine leaves*,[3] and drunk um to kill myself, 'cause Mast. Joe's Dina won't marry me."

This was an explanation of all the affair; the bull vine is a weed that grows in many of the Southern States, and possesses strong narcotic or stupefying properties; what its botanical name is I can't tell; this is all the name by which I have ever heard it called. The *intended* post-mortem is all that saved him; he was nearly gone; but when the blood commenced running, his brain was relieved of the engorgement, and he was aroused, more especially by the saw ripping across his bony simblin.[4]

I was then requested to go up to the house to see the old gentleman himself, as he had been sick for a day or two. After some few directions about Dick and his head, I went up and found the old fellow quite ill. The first thing on docket was to talk about Dick; I explained everything, I believe, to his entire satisfaction, more especially when I told him I thought Dick would recover. I then examined his condition, and found him suffering with an attack of pneumonia. I told him it was of a serious nature unless taken in time, and said that I thought he should be bled. He told me he had been bled, and the pain still continued. I proposed to him that he should be cupped on the side,[5] where the pain was.

On examination, I found he had been blistered on the part. I concluded I could find room sufficient to apply a few cups, and made preparation to do so. When I had everything ready I took up one and applied it near—Fire! murder! oh! John, take him off! Doctor! water! how did it come? where are you? eh? ha! oh whack! and he jumped some four or five feet high, with his hand clasped tight on the glass, and fell flat on his back in the middle of the floor.

In my haste and his fear, I had applied the cup to the recently blistered surface, which was as raw as a beef-steak. The way he squalled, rolled, kicked, puked, snorted, and sailed into the air, was a caution to old women on three legs. The remedy acted as a powerful revulsive, and after it was removed he felt *much better*.

When I had fixed him off and he had in a degree recovered his natural feelings, he told me he had a negro suffering with sore eyes, that he wanted me to see; sent for him, and had him brought to his own room. I examined his eyes and found them much inflamed and requiring remedial means immediately. I told him the negro should take a good purgative, live on spare diet, stay in the house out of the strong light, and be cupped on the temples. The cups were all ready, and I put the negro on a chair, scarified his temples, and now I was ready to apply them. I picked up one, fixed the dry paper and spirits, and all being nicely arranged, I proceeded to apply one. It is quick work, you know, and as the spirits and paper flashed in a blaze, while applying the cup, the negro jerked his head a little the wrong way, and—

"Lordy God! massa—poor nigga! my eye! coon skins! my ole tow britches! oh—oh!"

The cupping glass was over his eyes, and out it popped slick as a peeled onion. There now, I have done it, haint I? The nigger's eye was sucked out of joint before you could say Commodore Perry with your mouth shut.[6] I did not know what to do. I had heard many long lectures, read hundreds of pages of surgery, and had a little *common* sense myself, but this was a case I had never come across before nor behind either. If I went to pull off the cup as in ordinary cases, I would pull out the eyeball and all together: if I took something and broke glass, like fools do on all occasions, the pieces of glass would probably cut the eye so much that it would be lost.

What you reckon you'd done; done like me, I s'pose. I wanted the glass off and it had to come off or I would have been mobbed, or shot; just the same in Dutch, you see;[7] the negro shouting, jumping, foaming at the mouth like a mad dog; the old man crying out, "What in the devil have you done, doctor?" and—and—well, never mind the other things the nigger did; you know how people do when they get in a tight place sometimes, when they are scared. I picked up a hammer and knocked it into a hundred pieces. Cruel treatment, best I could do, though. The eye was a little worsted instead of relieved by the application. It went back in its place, and I concluded I was in just about scrapes enough for one day, and let the other eye alone for awhile, and trusted to internal remedies, such as small doses of tartar emetic, diluent drinks,[8] and purgatives. I toddled off home about this time.

I wish you may take my arm for a fish pole, my nose for a coffee-spout, my shins for dough-beaters, my ribs for toothpicks, and my all for a fool, if they didn't all get well. Roll up your sleeves to your knees, your breeches above your elbows, and come at me like the landlady of a boarding-house after her pay every Saturday morning. Here we go, all in a crowd by myself. Good-bye.

CHAPTER XVIII

A FIGHT WITH WOLVES

Air—Last tooth is broken that bound me to thee.

> *The night was dark, the wind did blow,*
> *But doctor, doctor, you must go;*
> *For far in yonder forest lies*
> *A man in pain, with sorrow cries.*
> *Yes, go I will, though hard it be*
> *To seek with wolves my destiny;*
> *And ere I shall return again,*
> *Your missus will of me complain.*

OLE JAW-BONE.

NOT long after the scenes described in the last chapter occurred, I was called up one night at eleven o'clock, to visit a patient fifteen miles off. It was a bitter pill, but I had to take it. The way we had to go was through a very bad swamp, and there was but two or three houses on the way, which would make it much more lonely and unpleasant, from the fact that the swamp was infested by all manner of wild beasts that roved the wild woods of the

southern and western country. We started, and well do I remember yet some of the sad reflections of that dreary night as I followed the negro that had come for me. Is this to be some of my
rewards for studying months and years; enduring hardships, un-
dergoing privations, and dragging out a life of toil and misery for
the sake of a living? Why was it that I secluded myself in bygone
days from the society of those that were most calculated to make
one happy; the young, the beautiful, amiable and accomplished
young ladies? Why was it that I left my native home and went to
dwell in a land of strangers? Why was it that I bade adieu to my
early associations, and parted with nearest and dearest friends?
Was it that I was to go day by day, and night by night, through
every danger and every inclemency of weather? that I was to be
hovering under my own shadow, while scorched with the burning rays of the sun, and that I was to stand alone and uncared for
in the depths of the forest, with nothing to protect me from the
beating rains and raging storm? Finding that such melancholy
thoughts would not change my condition, I struck up a conversation with the negro that was with me, about the patient that I was
going to see. He said it was "de bone-rattle ager, and dat if he
had one more, his massa said him must die."[1]

There is a very common saying in these parts to this day, and
in some other parts too, perhaps, I can't tell, that a fellow never
has but three of those congestive chills, or "bone rattle agers," as
they are commonly called here. Whether there is anything in the
number three or not, I don't pretend to say, but one thing is certain, that persons scarcely ever survive the third paroxysm, and
as the negro's master had been called out twice, he very reason-
ably concluded that the next turn would be his last, unless he got
a doctor in time. Oh, ye sons of Esculapius, how long will it be
until your worth is known, your services appreciated? You will
all no doubt remember many cases similar to the one that I am
now relating, in which the friends and the patient would cry out,
"Oh, doctor, if you cure me how grateful I shall feel; how punc-

tually I will pay you; what a friend I will prove;" and as soon as they are again restored to health and happiness, these have been the first to behold you with a careless, a scornful look; none readier to dispute a reasonable bill, and for no cause denounce your name in every crowd on every occasion. But as this is the order of the day, let us bear it the best we can, though I know from sad experience how such things have often caused a feeling of emotion to rise in your breast.

We were going along talking about the case, and not thinking of danger, when we were suddenly startled by our horses becoming alarmed, and before we had time to imagine what was the cause, we were both flumpuxed like a dab of fat on the ground, and our horses going off at the rate of twenty-five miles an hour. The negro was thrown some ten steps ahead of me, and as he struck the ground I heard him commence hollowing like he was killed. Not knowing what I would have to do when I got to him, I concluded I had as well go with a knife and pistol in hand, as a box of pills and tooth-pullers. I put my hand in the pocket where I always kept my pistol, and to my awful disappointment it was gone. I then ran my hand in a side pocket for my big knife, and if it wasn't gone too you may kill me. Where had I lost them; where had I left them; what had become of them? I certainly had not left them at home; something I never forgot, equally as necessary as my saddle-bags full of medicines. What was I to do in this dilemma? the negro hallooing for "Help, help, massa, for God's sake! wolf eat poor nigga up—oh! my head."

I didn't know what to do; I knew I could do nothing with a wolf without weapons; my horse was gone, and if the wolves killed the negro they would next commence on me. I was so scared that I didn't know whether the deuce had me or whether I was drunk, and forgot for a moment that I had been thrown from my horse; but when I did think of it, I got to looking around and feeling as fast as if I was on hot iron, trying to find my pistol and knife. They were the first things I laid my hands on, and as I

As soon as I caught a glimpse of them, I let one of them have it in the short ribs with all the force of gunpowder.

grabbed them I ran up to see what sort of a fix the negro was in. He was in a tolerably tight place, *he was,* for there I saw two whaling big wolves, as large as a year old calf, diving into the negro's head and neck with as much composure as eating fried dogs' tails.

As soon as I caught a glimpse of them, I let one of them have it in the short ribs with all the force of gunpowder. He tumbled off like he didn't know what hurt him. The other wolf showed no disposition to loose his hold, and as he would in all *brutal* probability, eat into the nigger's provision box before I could reload my pistol in the dark, I thought it best to go at him with my knife. I went up to him with a rush, and made a lick at him, which fortunately struck him, but not fortunately enough, for he left the negro and thought he'd just walk into a little of my tender meat. He came at me like Bill come out of the watermelon patch, in a mighty hurry, made a spring and lit right on my head. His weight made me cave in, and down I fell on the ground, with the wolf on top of me. As I fell I made a swipe at him, and put my steel into his stomach and bowels astonishing. The blood gushed out, but still he gnawed the faster on my head. One more attempt and I put my knife to his heart, thus ridding myself of a load of wolf and sin too tedious to mention. The old negro, true to his preserver, was up, ready and willing to assist me. He had received some severe wounds in the back, head, and shoulders, and my own pate had a good chawin' also.

We viewed our fallen enemies for a moment in silence, and then looked around for our horses, my saddle-bags, &c. The saddle-bags were soon found, but the horses were gone. Rather a desirable situation to be placed in, three miles from nowhere, and the same distance from any other town. I told the negro that his horse was to blame, for mine had never been guilty of such a mean thing by himself. The negro put my saddle-bags across his shoulders, and we went on to the house of the patient. We arrived about daylight, and found the horses there, with saddle and all safe. The old man's chill was expected between ten and eleven o'clock that day. I went to work to prevent a recurrence by giving large doses of quinine, keeping him well covered in bed, hot irons to his feet, and, as the time drew near, occasionally a little hot brandy toddy.[2] By these means he passed the time in safety, sweating like a sugar-house.[3] I told him to take a little quinine the next day, be careful for a short time, and he would soon be able to eat like a thrashing machine.[4] Thus far all things went on well, and before leaving, I went with the gentleman's wife to take some dinner under a shelter in the yard. I was sitting at the table eating, and talking of the difference between living in the backwoods and in a city or older settled country. I told her there was a vast difference; that in the city or old country we could go to church, have a great many luxuries and comforts of life, calculated to make one happy and contented, that we could not meet with in a newly settled country like that.

"Yes," she said, "I recollect how I used to enjoy myself, but I ran away and married, and had to come out here; but I've got accustomed to—ouch!—hu—e!—snakes!—run here—everybody."

I jumped up, overset the table in my fright, and run to the other side to see what so much noise was for. The poor woman didn't halloo for nothing, for there were some half dozen snakes as long as a clothes pole, and as big as your leg, running after her every way she went. She was screaming for life or help one; and I would have risked anything to save her, for if I hadn't she would not send for me again. I was not very stout, and she was not very heavy; so I picked her up to get her out of reach of the snakes, and ran with her a few steps to put her on what I thought to be a wash-tub on a big stump with the bottom upward, but which turned out to be a tub brimming full of soft soap, set up there to cool. She screamed a little louder than ever, gave one kick, and down her and the tub of soap all came on me, and I flat on my back. By this time the negroes had killed the snakes, and she and I took a good washing.

I was very happy to find that the soap was not hot, or we would have been in a worse fix still. During the excitement her husband could not lie in bed, but got up while in a good sweat and ran out to see what was the matter. I reckon he thought I was trying to kill his wife or something else, but I wasn't. Poor man! he paid dear for getting up contrary to the doctor's orders one time, but he won't again. His getting up brought the chill on him at last. He struggled, his wife struggled, and I struggled with him for two long hours but it was all to no purpose; he fixed up his things and went straight along off to the next world.

CHAPTER XIX

HOW TO CURE DEAFNESS
IN THREE HOURS

Air—Will you meet me at the black stump?

How sad the thought that one is deaf,
And tries in vain to get relief.
They're dead to all the sweetest sounds,
Which causes grief that has no bounds;
But when all things in vain are tried,
There seems no hope that's left beside.
Still trying, you may find a man
Who will relieve you at command.

JOHNNY DOG-TAIL.

A few months after curing the man that had a snake in his digestive ballot-box, he was at a neighbor's house and they got to talking about a negro that his neighbor had that had been deaf for several years; consequently he was much reduced in *value*.[1] The owner of the negro said that he thought the negro was "possuming" of it,[2] and could hear as well as anybody. He had taken him to a noted doctor in Mississippi, and to this place, that, and the other, and all did no good. Old Tom Dupree (the snake man) told him that if any man in the world—or any other place, could cure the negro that Dr. Rattlehead could, whether he was deaf or not, and told him to give me a trial anyhow, for, said old Tom, "He cured me after every hope of recovery was given up." His neighbor promised him that he would go and see me the first chance.

A few days after this I was up at *Shake-rag,* a little cross-road of a place that we called "town,"—double handsfull of dry goods, and *cotton hankerchers,* an old blacksmith shop, and a barrel of whisky. Well, here I saw the man that had the deaf negro. Old Tom brought him up and told him I was the great doctor he had been speaking of, and commenced about the deaf negro. I had heard nothing of it before, and was not prepared very well to tell him whether I could cure the negro or not. He told me he had long had his doubts whether Jack was deaf or not, from the way it came on him. One evening he had given him a good frailing about something, and next morning he got up with his hand to his ear, as deaf as a rich man to the cries of the needy, and had never heard a lick since. I asked him to send for the negro, and I would soon tell him whether I could cure him or not. He did so. The negro came up and I examined, and could *see* nothing in his ears to make him deaf, and from the way the negro acted and looked at me I thought he was doin' up the rascal very brown. I took his master off a few steps and asked him if he had tried whipping the negro; he said yes, but it did no good. Says I to him, if you will give me twenty-five dollars I will make your negro hear as well in two days as he ever did, or I will charge you nothing. He said he would give it. We then went back where the negro was; I motioned the negro to follow me, and I went into the woods where no person was near—and now for putting Jack to the test. I commenced talking to him as though he could hear as well as anybody.

"Sit down, Jack," and he did it without another word and without any motions, as he was used to. I saw I had him by the leg at once. I continued—

"Well, Jack, I know you can hear as well as I can, but I don't blame you for treating your old master so, for he whips and knocks poor negroes about just like dogs; I brought you out here, not to beat you, but to have a little talk with you about getting free. I live in a free State when I am at home, and have come here to take all the black folks to a free State; and now, if you want to go with me and be free, tell me whether you can hear good enough to come to-night at the back of the turnip patch when I whistle? all the other—"

"God bless you, massa, I hear good as any nigga; me come any time."

"Very well," says I, "you have your things ready tonight, so we can start as soon as the white folks get to sleep, and when I whistle by the *black stump,* in the turnip patch, after bedtime, you come out, and when you hear me say, 'that you, Jack?' you must say, 'yes, here me, massa.'"

Jack understood and agreed to all. I told him not to let anyone know that he could hear until he came to my call at night. We then went on back to where we had left his master.

"Well, Doctor, what do you think of Jack?"

"I am very sorry that I can not do anything for him."

He sent Jack on home. I told him I wanted him and one other man to go with me that night a little distance, and I would show them a sight worth looking at. He wanted to know what I was going to do.

"That's nothing to you, I want you to go, and promise you that nothing shall hurt either of you: is that not sufficient?"

He agreed to go. We all went on to his house, had our horses fed, got supper, and were sitting comfortably at the fire smoking out of a cobpipe, and enjoying ourselves in talking of things in general, nothing in particular, until I said to him, "Now, sir, lay down the pipes, get you and your man ready, and let's be off."

We were soon ready, and I told them they were not to speak a word after leaving the house until I spoke to them. We started out, and I led them to the appointed place. When we got there I whispered to them to sit down behind the stump. I stood for a few moments before attempting any movements. I could hear them breathing, and their hearts beating like they thought I was going to murder them. After waiting for everything to get still, I gave the whistle. Jack was ready and waiting for the glad sound, and here he came walking as large as life.

"That you, Jack?"

"Yes, here me, massa."

"Come on, Jack."

"I cum, sir."

"Mr. Jordan," said I, "*here is your negro cured of deafness.*"

He saw how I had managed, and got a little of the maddest that I ever saw a man in my life, and cried out,

"Is that you, Jack?"

"My God! dar's ole massa!"

Jordan stepped out to meet Jack, but he took to his heels and did his cleanest best to get away, but they overhauled him, and if he didn't get one good slashing, then a negro never got one since Adam turned 'em out of the garden. I made Jordan fork over the twenty-five, and I left for home while things were right end upward.

CHAPTER XX

RATTLEHEAD'S
FAREWELL ADDRESS

Air—A life in the woods.

Farewell, good folks, now I must leabe you,
You am tired, an' so is me too;
I's told some scrapes dat I am bin in,
Ob bars, an' wolves, an' de coons a grinnin';
But me, poor fellar, am had bad luck
Dat's gin my system a mighty shuck.
So dis volume will git no bigger nor less,
After Rattlehead's farewell address.

THE DOCTOR HIMSELF.

I AM now about to draw my history to a close, and, my dear reader, you can not imagine what a solemn feeling it puts on me to write these closing lines. Yes, when I think that this volume is to be read by many that may doubt my veracity, that it is to be in the hands of many that do not know anything of backwoods life and that it will be viewed by the eye of critics, I can but feel its influence. I had intended to give you a more lengthy history, and could fill three such volumes, but I am prevented by a sad misfortune that has befallen me; and, as the last tribute of respect that I may ever have the opportunity of paying to the departed ones, I will presently give you an account of it. It may awaken in your hearts one feeling of sympathy and sorrow. Had this accident not happened, I intended giving you an account of my attendance on my second course of lectures (which was in one of the large eastern cities), my difficulties in getting my diploma, my scrapes through the winter, on my return to Arkansaw, and many other things that would have been interesting; but I must close now to attend to other duties devolving on me, and which I cannot neglect; and hope, in the course of twelve months, that I will have an opportunity of giving my remaining history! and if so, you shall then hear all about why I have had to close before completing my life. And now, before giving you an account of the sad accident, let me bid you adieu, and let me hope that your course in life will be smoother than mine has been, and may you never have to drink of the cup of sorrow as I have done: may you never have to weep over hopes deceived, love betrayed, and plighted pledges broken, friendship abused, confidence violated, and the heart's warmest affection blasted, as I have done; but may your life be one of uninterrupted happiness, and may your sky ever remain unclouded, and you all remain as I find you, the happiest of beings, is the wish of your friend,

Rattlehead.

Mr. Hanly, of whom I have so often spoken in the course of this work, has been one of the best friends that I have ever met with in life. His family was composed of himself and lady and two daughters: they were both young, beautiful, and amiable, and though reared up in the rude state of society incident to newly settled countries, and not situated where they could have the advantage of becoming accomplished, kinder hearts never beat in human breast than in theirs: more devoted and affectionate beings never lived. Yes, they have been as sisters to me since my stay at their father's house; they have ministered to my wants, and cooled the burning brow when scorched with fever. But I must proceed. One afternoon Mr. Hanly, his youngest daughter, and myself, rode out some six miles to a sulphur spring that we were in the habit of visiting every few days. Now you are thinking I was in love with her: you are mistaken; I loved both the young ladies like sisters, as friends and nothing more. Remember Mollie that died long ago. Well, we went to the spring a little later than usual, and did not have long to stay. We were on our return home, and were talking, I believe, about how I happened to come to Arkansas. Mr. Hanly was riding before, the young lady next to him, and I in the rear. We had to ride this way as there was nothing but a path through the woods. We were within three miles of home, and all in fine spirits, happy and contented, not dreaming that a silent foe was in ambush for us. We traveled on until we got under a large tree that leaned over the path, and, sudden as the lightning's flash, I was filled with horror at the shriek of poor Miss Julia. A large panther sprung from the bending tree, and fell with terrific force upon her. As she saw the panther descending, she screamed out, "Oh, father!" and by the time the words were uttered, she was crushed to the earth.

Her father was quickly to her side, and endeavored to save his child from danger. The horse she was riding being frightened, ran off with all speed, and her father jumping off of his, to save her, his horse also ran off. What a scene to behold! The panther, as he leaped, caught her throat in his mouth. Mr. Hanly seeing this took out his large knife and endeavored to pierce the animal to the heart: he made one lick at him, and failing to inflict a fatal wound, the panther turned on him, and threw him to the ground. How did it happen that my horse was worse scared than I ever saw him? Oh! would that it had been otherwise! but it was so; he took fright, and before I could stop him or get off, he ran more than fifty yards. I jumped off and ran up to save my friends.

When I got within about ten steps of them, I saw the panther on Mr. Hanly, tearing his flesh to pieces, and Miss Julia lying near him. I thought that I was too late, but I had done my best to get there sooner. I went within four or five steps of them, took out my pistol and fired at the panther. It was a fatal shot, but fearing it was not, I run my knife to the hilt in his side, and he fell dead at my feet. I then turned to Mr. Hanly and his daughter; it was too late; the animal had killed Miss Julia, no doubt, when he fell on her, his teeth and the force of the blow being sufficient to fracture the bones of her neck. Mr. Hanly was lying there with the blood gushing from his wounds; he still had some life in him but it was almost extinct; he called me; I went to him, he said to me—

"Is Julia killed?"

I told him I thought she was.

"Well, Doc., you see I am going in a few moments, let me say to you, tell my wife farewell for me," the tears streaming from his large black eyes as he said it; "don't let her and Mary suffer."

I told him they should never suffer while I lived.

"Farewell, Doc., I'm most gone."

I tried to staunch the blood, it was in vain; the caroted artery[1] was wounded. He offered up some feeble prayer, again he said "Farewell, Doc." I held his hand in mine, I felt his pulse, it was sinking fast. Again he committed his wife and daughter to my care. He whispered something which I could not understand. His noble heart fluttered, it ceased to beat; he is gone from time to eternity! It was an awful sight; my best friend on earth was gone. After waiting a few moments I got up, turned round, and there stood my horse. I went for the nearest neighbor, and we managed to get them home by night. It was a heart-sickening scene to behold that wife and daughter, when they saw those lifeless forms before them. I consoled them all I could. Next day they were buried. And now my sad account is given; my friends are gone, they are safely housed in heaven, free from all the sorrows and cares of life.

NOTES

THE annotations given in the notes are provided as an aid to readers of this edition of *The Life and Adventures of an Arkansaw Doctor* and are not considered exhaustive. I have generally sought to provide notes where I thought they would be of help and to refrain from those which seem to be overly intrusive and thus detract from enjoyment of the book. The motif numbers cited are from Stith Thompson's *Motif-Index of Folk Literature* (Bloomington: Indiana University Press, 1955–58), one of the standard indices used by folklorists to determine the folk currency of various narrative elements.

W. K. M.

Introduction

1. James R. Masterson, "The Arkansaw Doctor," *Annals of Medical History,* 3d ser., 2 (1940): 30. Masterson also briefly discusses Byrn's life and career in *Arkansas Folklore: The Arkansas Traveler, Davey Crockett, and Other Legends* (1942; reprint, Little Rock: Rose Publishing Co., 1974), pp. 88–91.

2. Masterson, "The Arkansaw Doctor," p. 30.

3. *Ibid.*

4. See p. 4 of the present edition.

5. Masterson, "The Arkansaw Doctor," p. 31.

6. This proclamation is made in an advertisement on the back of Byrn's *Ragged Edge Rambles* (New York: M. L. Byrn, 1882) and refers to his entire series of humorous works.

7. This pamphlet was apparently issued sometime before 1857; it is

mentioned as a "prize essay" in another pamphlet published that year. Later references refer to it as a lecture available in print for ten cents. It was reprinted in *The Farmer's Friend and Home Companion. Comprising a Treatise on the Management of Bees. Also Numerous Recipes of Great Value to Farmers, Manufacturers and Others. Also—a Lecture on Tobacco.* (New York: M. L. Byrn, 1868), pp. 11–17.

8. The two pamphlets are *The Al-ma-kan-tur Circle, and Calendar of Love. Containing Revelations and Mysteries, Facts and New Discoveries, Never Before Offered to the Public, Being of the Greatest Importance to Both Married and Single Persons, of Both Sexes* (New York: M. L. Byrn, 1857); and *The Physiology of Marriage and Philosophy of Generation, Being a Confidential and Reliable Friend for Medical and Scientific Consultation, on Subjects of Vital Importance* (New York: M. L. Byrn, 1863). The quotation is from *The Physiology of Marriage,* pp. 11–12.

9. This six-page essay first appeared in *The Al-ma-kan-tur Circle* (1857) and was subsequently published in nine of Byrn's other publications. The quote here is from *The Al-ma-kan-tur Circle,* p. 119.

10. M. L. Byrn, *The Singing Evangelist* (New York: M. L. Byrn, 1888), pp. 6–8.

11. Masterson transcribed these "Rules for Life" from a manuscript in the possession of Mrs. Charles J. Stevenson, Baldwin, Long Island, New York; Mrs. Stevenson was Byrn's daughter. Masterson, "The Arkansaw Doctor," p. 36.

12. Byrn's licensing as an "Exhorter" occurred at Washington Square Church, New York, on August 5, 1861.

13. This is the same advertisement referred to in note six above.

14. *Phudge Phumble's Fillossofy of Phoolishness. A Perpetual Komic Kallender, phor the Present and the Phutre. A Phoreteller of Past Events, and Kronikle of Things in General, phor the Benephit of Evry Boddy, or the Balance of Human Kind and Wimmin Tew. Warranted Not to Kutt in the Ey. Writt by Phudge Phumble, M.D. Awthur oph "Lov Scrapes of a Lyphe Tyme," "Rambles of Phudge Phumble in Search of a Wife," "Arkansaw Doktur," "Rattlehead's Kronikles," & So 4th, and So On (Cash in Advance and No Questions Asked)* (New York: M. L. Byrn, 1880), p. 5.

15. *Ibid.,* p. 7.

16. David Rattlehead, *Rattlehead's Chronicles; or, a Little Experience with*

Old Maids and Young Maids; Old Bachelors, Fools, and Drunkards; Quack Doctors, Men of Science, and the World at Large (Philadelphia: Lippincott, Grambo & Co., 1852), p. 22.

17. See chapter 4 of the present edition.
18. See chapter 9, especially pp. 60–64, of the present edition.
19. See p. 109 of the present edition.
20. See p. 117 of the present edition.
21. See p. 133 of the present edition.
22. See chapter 16 of the present edition.
23. See p. 28 of the present edition.
24. See p. 89 of the present edition.
25. See note 9 to chapter 12 of the present edition.
26. See p. 105 and note 8 for chapter 14 of the present edition.
27. See p. 105 of the present edition.
28. See p. 64 and note 8 for chapter 9 of the present edition.
29. *Widow-woman* appears on p. 74 of the present edition; *diggins* on p. 75; *hain't* on p. 65.
30. See p. 105 and note 11 for chapter 14 of the present edition.
31. See p. 26 of the present edition.
32. The phrase "as still as death" is found on p. 5 of the present edition; "as white as snow" on p. 105; "Old Harry" on p. 18; and "it always killed or cured" on p. 71.
33. The saying "certain as three ones make a broomstick" appears on p. 8 of the present edition; "as plain as an ugly man sees his own beauty" on p. 16; "like a blind dog in a meat-house" on p. 13.
34. See p. 22 of the present edition.
35. The phrase "played thunder with" appears on p. 17 of the present edition; "drunk as a fool" on p. 13.
36. Bennett Wood Green, *Word-Book of Virginia Folk-Speech* (1899; reprint, New York: Benjamin Blom, 1971), p. 19.
37. Bell Irvin Wiley, *The Common Soldier in the Civil War: The Life of Billy Yank* (New York: Grosset & Dunlap, 1952), p. 187.
38. See p. 42 and note 1 for chapter 6 of the present edition.
39. See chapter 3 of the present edition.
40. See chapter 10 of the present edition.
41. See chapter 6 of the present edition.

42. See chapter 9, especially p. 66, of the present edition. For a discussion of the fight scene as found in Southwestern humor see Joseph J. Arpad, "The Fight Story: Quotation and Originality in Native American Humor," *Journal of the Folklore Institute* 10 (1973): 141–172.

43. See chapter 5, especially p. 37, of the present edition.

44. See p. 37 of the present edition.

45. See p. 62 of the present edition.

46. See p. 63 of the present edition.

Preface

1. The noun *bolus* is used in veterinary medicine to refer to a large pill. Byrn evidently uses the word here to make a humorous comment, for he was a physician, not a veterinarian.

2. Possibly this is a fictitious name, but most of those who have commented on Rattlehead's book think it may actually refer to a place in Mississippi County or Crittenden County, Arkansas. This place name does not appear on any map of Arkansas that I have been able to find. It is possible that some present Arkansas town once bore this name, but, if so, the name change occurred many decades ago. Byrn's daughter, the late Mrs. Charles J. Stevenson of Baldwin, Long Island, told James R. Masterson that she often heard her father speak of Raccoon Bayou as a real place in Arkansas, near the Mississippi River. See James R. Masterson, "The Arkansaw Doctor," *Annals of Medical History,* 3d ser., 2 (1940): 49; idem, *Tall Tales of Arkansaw* (Boston: Chapman & Grimes, 1942), p. 335.

Chapter I

1. As explained in the introduction to this edition, these introductory verses are generally considered to be products of Byrn's imagination, possibly parodies of then popular songs.

2. Dr. Byrn was born at Statesville, Wilson County, Tennessee, on September 4, 1826. See the introduction to this edition. Also see

Masterson, *Tall Tales of Arkansaw,* p. 334; idem, "The Arkansaw Doctor," p. 30.

3. It is possible that Byrn's *"log-cabin" education* is a reference to informal instruction. The use of *sisters* here is evidently intended as a humorous replacement for *brothers,* a cliché commonly used to refer to fellow human beings. It may also be a reference to the fact that Byrn was instructed along with his sisters. According to Masterson ("The Arkansaw Doctor," p. 30), Byrn did attend some sort of formal secondary school; perhaps *log-cabin* merely refers to the type of building in which the school was housed.

4. The proverbial phrase "as still as death" has been around for several centuries and has been popular with American writers since at least the eighteenth century. One of its first appearances in print was in William Bartram's *Travels Through North and South Carolina, Georgia, East and West Florida* (1791), although it was certainly in common use prior to the 1790s. Sally Wister noted the saying in 1778 in her *Journal,* Albert C. Myers, ed. (Philadelphia, 1902). See Bartlett Jere Whiting, *Early American Proverbs and Proverbial Phrases* (Cambridge, Massachusetts: Harvard University Press, 1977), p. 98. For uses of the phrase in the nineteenth century, see Archer Taylor and Bartlett Jere Whiting, *A Dictionary of American Proverbs and Proverbial Phrases 1820–1880* (Cambridge, Massachusetts: Harvard University Press, 1967), p. 95; Jan Harold Brunvand, *A Dictionary of Proverbs and Proverbial Phrases from Books Published by Indiana Authors Before 1890* (Bloomington, Indiana: Indiana University Press, 1961), p. 34.

5. During the era Byrn is writing about it was customary for travelers to stay in private homes when they were in a rural region at nightfall.

6. Morpheus is the god of dreams in Greek mythology; hence, falling into the arms of Morpheus refers to going to sleep.

7. The phrase "knocked into a cocked hat" was very popular in nineteenth-century American literature. One of its first printed appearances was in the 1834 volume of uncertain authorship, *A Narrative of the Life of David Crockett.* For references to the phrase's appearance in this era, see Taylor and Whiting, p. 173.

8. Byrn's description of this Negro follows the stereotypical depic-

tion of blacks common throughout the nineteenth century. Various entertainment media of the era portrayed black men as big and menacing with enormous mouths and eyes that seemed to be perpetually rolling. One volume devoted to these stereotypes as they have existed in popular songs throughout American history is Sam Dennison's *Scandalize My Name: Black Imagery in American Popular Music* (New York: Garland Publishing, Inc., 1982).

9. The panorama was an especially popular form of entertainment in the nineteenth century. It was a picture or series of pictures of a landscape, historical event, or some other scenery presented on a continuous surface encircling the spectator. Thus, to say that the Negro rolled his eyes like a panorama means that he rolled them in a very wide arc.

10. This is probably a saying that Byrn made up, for it does not appear in any proverb dictionary.

11. This once common practice of marketing is described by Thomas D. Clark in his *The Southern Country Store: Pills, Petticoats, & Plows* (1944; reprint, Norman, Oklahoma: University of Oklahoma Press, 1974), p. 275:

Every merchant selected a Price Symbol as soon as he went into business, and it was made a password to his sales methods. It had to contain ten letters, preferably no two alike, and it could not be too easy to decipher. Some of these were "Baltimore," "Comb basket," "Black Snake," "Prudential," "Cumberland," the first ten letters of the greek alphabet, and special [i.e. invented] symbols . . . Thus markings on goods became "XXZV" or $14.00. Always it was the practice to mark goods with both the purchase and selling prices. If a store did an appreciable cash business, clerks marked the purchase, cash, and credit prices. In this way the trade was unable to keep up with values. One of the favorite pastimes for the few customers who understood the use of code words was that of trying to guess what they meant.

12. This is probably another saying that Byrn made up; it does not appear in any proverb dictionary.

13. For various appearances of this proverb in nineteenth-century American literature see Taylor and Whiting, p. 354.

14. Queensware is glazed earthenware of a creamy color.

15. Blue mass is a purgative made from a combination of quicksilver and confection of roses. Such pills were a staple of country doctors

in nineteenth-century America. See, for example, John Quincy Wolf, *Life in the Leatherwoods* (1974; reprint, Little Rock: August House, 1988), p. 100.

16. A pun on the word *masonry* and Freemasonry; the latter is usually referred to colloquially as Masonry or Masons. Squares, of course, are symbolic of organization and construction. According to Masonic tradition the order had its origin in the East and carried the arts and sciences of civilization to the West. Members of the Freemasons are bound by oath not to reveal the secrets of their society; Byrn's pun here hinges on the reader understanding the secret nature of Freemasonry.

17. For nineteenth-century usages of the proverbial phrase "played thunder with" see Taylor and Whiting, p. 372. Byrn's inclusion of the phrase in this book is the earliest known usage.

18. *Thunder-mug* is a slang term for a chamberpot.

19. That is, money.

20. The phrase "like a blind dog in a meat-house" seems to be original with Byrn although it could be a saying that he heard which has otherwise gone unreported. There are, of course, many other traditional sayings and phrases involving a dog simile. For several references to appearances of the proverbial phrase "drunk as a fool" in nineteenth-century literature see Taylor and Whiting, p. 142. The phrase first appeared in print in Thomas A. Burke's *Polly Peablossom's Wedding and Other Tales* (1851) and in the present work. It almost certainly predates the 1850s, for the phrase is cited in Bennett Wood Green's *Word-Book of Virginia Folk-Speech* (1899; reprint, New York: Benjamin Blom, 1971), p. 19, as a word of some antiquity and is quoted in Bell I. Wiley's *The Life of Billy Yank* (Indianapolis: The Bobbs-Merrill Company, Inc., 1952), p. 187, as a familiar phrase used by Union soldiers in their letters home. A muster is a gathering of troops for inspection and, in the first half of the nineteenth century, was loosely applied to general training days. These were monthly drill gatherings of men who were ordered by law to serve in the local militia.

21. In Greek and Roman mythology Bacchus, also known as Dionysus, the son of Zeus (Jupiter) and Semele, was the god of wine and revelry. Thus, to "dive into Bacchus" means to partake of intoxicating drinks.

Chapter II

1. Galen (130–200) was a Greek physician and writer whose writings were the principal element of the curriculum in medical schools of the Middle Ages. Galen's authority was seriously questioned during the Renaissance, but his ideas were so deeply rooted by then that it took centuries for them to be totally replaced. Even as late as 1900 there were many "Neogalenists."

2. This is, apparently, another example of a proverbial comparison invented by Byrn. It appears in no proverb collections.

3. *Wormwood* refers to any of several related strong-smelling plants of the genus *Artemisia,* with white or yellow flowers, or specifically to *Artemisia absinthium,* a species that secretes a bitter-tasting, dark-green oil used in making absinthe. *Gall* refers to a bitter, slightly alkaline, yellowish-green fluid secreted in the glandular substance of the liver and stored in the gall bladder. In general use it usually refers to anything bitter or distasteful; this is the sense used by Byrn.

4. The phrase "starting off on the right foot," or some variation of it, was quite popular in nineteenth-century literature. In J. M. Potts et al, eds., *Journals and Letters of Francis Asbury* (London, 1958) 2:576, which dates from 1808, Asbury speaks of putting "the wrong foot foremost." The *Letters of John Randolph to a Young Relative* (1834) contain an entry dated 1822 referring to a "Mr. Speaker B." who "set off wrong foot foremost." For other appearances of the phrase in nineteenth-century literature, see Taylor and Whiting, p. 143; Brunvand, p. 53. Most references use the form "put the best foot forward" rather than "starting off on the right foot." Sometimes, of course, the reference is to the right or best leg.

5. The slang term *Old Harry* is a reference to the Devil; it is of fairly ancient usage. The term probably comes from a mixture called Old Harry that was used at one time by vintners who wished to spoil their wines. The term first appeared in print in 1810 but is probably much older. For several instances of the term, see Taylor and Whiting, p. 269; J. S. Farmer and W. E. Henley, *Slang and Its Analogues* (1890–1904; reprint, New York: Arno Press, Inc., 1970), V:97. The phrase "play the Old Harry" means, of course, to play the devil. The English

naval officer and novelist Frederick Marryat was one of the first to pub-
lish the phrase in this verb form when he used it in his *Dog Friend*
(1837).

6. Stubble is the stalk ends of wheat, rye, barley, oats, corn, etc., left
in the ground after harvesting. Such material would burn very quickly.

7. This is another example of a proverbial phrase that, apparently,
was made up by Byrn.

Chapter III

1. For a description of a Negro corn-shucking by a contemporary
of Byrn's, see David C. Barrow, Jr., "A Georgia Corn-Shucking," in
Bruce Jackson, ed., *The Negro and His Folklore in Nineteenth-Century Peri-
odicals* (Austin: University of Texas Press, 1967), pp. 168–176; first
published in *Century Magazine* (1882).

2. The proverbial phrase "laid in the shade" first appeared in print
in Johnson J. Hooper's *Some Adventures of Captain Simon Suggs* (1845),
published six years before Byrn's book. For its other appearances in
nineteenth-century literature, see Taylor and Whiting, p. 323.

3. This is, evidently, Byrn's play on the proverbial phrase "as white
as a sheet," an old and well-known comparison. The humor hinges not
only on the unexpected word *sheet* but on the unlikelihood of a sheet
being black, at least a sheet that anyone was proud of.

4. This is a parody on the lines of "Sourwood Mountain," a Southern mountain tune that is known primarily as an instrumental number
rather than a vocal. The earliest reference by a folksong collector is in
Louise Rand Bascom, "Ballads and Songs of Western North Carolina,"
Journal of American Folklore 22 (April–June, 1909): 238–250. Just how
much it predates 1909 is uncertain, although Bryn's reference indicates
it dates back more than fifty years. Most lyric versions are short, generally consisting of no more than two or three verses. Vance Randolph
recorded a text from Joshua C. Keithley, Ridgedale, Missouri, August
26, 1940 (*Ozark Folksongs* [1946–1950; reprint, Columbia: University of
Missouri Press, 1980], 3:156). Keithley's two verses contain the following lines:

> Old man, old man, I want your daughter,
> Hi ho diddle dum, hi ho day,
> To make my bread an' pack my water,
> Hi ho diddle dum a day.

Even more relevant to the present discussion are two texts from *The Frank C. Brown Collection of North Carolina Folklore* (Durham: Duke University Press, 1952), 3:285. The first, reported in July, 1922, was collected from a Jennie Belvin of Durham:

> Old man, old man, what'll you take for your daughter?
> Fifteen cents, a dollar an' a quarter.

The second, contributed by a Mamie E. Cheek of Durham, consists of the following lines:

> Old man, old man, I want your daughter.
> Well you can have her for a dollar and a quarter.

The form reported by Byrn does not appear in any folklore collection and, while it is not impossible that the lines were in oral tradition, it seems likely that they are of the author's invention.

5. In Southern folk tradition, and often in nineteenth-century Southern fiction, a merchant was a greedy, unreliable character who only told the truth when it was beneficial to him.

6. This saying is usually reported as "as poor as Job's turkey" or "as mean as Job's turkey"; in no other printed source is the phrase "since Job killed the 'fat turkey'" reported. This is not necessarily proof that Byrn put this twist on the old phrase, but it is a good indication of the likelihood.

7. There are many references to someone moving like a streak of lightning, but the color blue is rarely used in most printed references. "Moffat's pills" probably refers to some patent medicine available in 1851. In Byrn's later *Rattlehead's Chronicles; or, a Little Experience with Old Maids and Young Maids; Old Bachelors, Fools, and Drunkards; Quack Doctors, Men of Science, and The World at Large* (1852), a book reissued in 1882 as *Ragged Edge Rambles,* he included mock advertisements for various patent medicines, one of which is Moffat's Life Pills (p. 47). It is

possible that Moffat's Life Pills was a fictitious name made up by Byrn to represent the genre, possibly as a means of avoiding a libel charge. At any rate, I have been unable to find any mention of them except that which is contained in the various publications of Dr. Byrn.

8. This is a reference to the cold water pledge that, when signed by alcoholics, was supposed to be irrefragable proof of their desire to remain teetotalers for the rest of their lives.

Chapter IV

1. That is, whether he wanted to be associated with Byrn or not.
2. At the time of which Byrn is writing there were no laws in America providing for the legal acquisition of human bodies for medical purposes. As a result, doctors and medical colleges frequently resorted to illegal means of obtaining cadavers for instructional and investigative purposes. Many doctors engaged in grave robbing themselves, as in the instance recounted by Byrn, or they depended on the services of professional thieves or grave robbers. Sometimes the corpse was stolen before interment, and sometimes a person was murdered by a professional criminal who then sold the body to a doctor or medical school. This latter craft was practiced infrequently, although it occurred often enough to inspire the verb *to burke*. This term, which means to murder in such a way as to leave few marks of violence, was named after an Irishman, William Burke, who with his partner, William Hare, did a thriving business as body-snatcher murderers in Edinburgh in the early nineteenth century. Only one case of burking has ever been reported in the United States. For more information on the subject, see Gladys-Marie Fry, *Night Riders in Black Folk History* (Knoxville: The University of Tennessee Press, 1975), pp. 176–177.

An interesting comment on the practice of doctors plundering graves for their cadavers is contained in this epitaph from Hoosick Falls, New York, reported in John R. Kippax, *Churchyard Literature: A Choice Collection of American Epitaphs with Remarks on Monumental Inscriptions and the Obsequies of Various Nations* (1876; reprint, Willliamstown, Massachusetts: Corner House Publishers, 1978), p. 171:

Ruth Sprague
Died 1846, aged 9 yrs. & 4 months.
She was stolen by Roderick R. Clow. Her body was dissected at the office of Dr. P. Armstrong, Hoosick, New York; where her mutilated remains were found and deposited here.

> Her body dissected by fiendish men,
> Her bones anatomized,
> Her soul—we trust—has risen to God,
> Where few physicians rise.

3. The phrase "until old 'Pidey's' horn grows off" is possibly a play on the saying "until Gabriel blows his horn." It is, in any case, not found in any proverb collection.

4. These references to Yankees, meaning residents of New England, and to tin peddlers reflect fashionable stereotypes of the 1850s. For more about popular attitudes towards tin peddlers, see Margaret Coffin, *The History & Folklore of American Country Tinware 1700–1900* (New York: Galahad Books, 1968), especially pp. 185–201.

5. Byrn means here that they were not able to accomplish much. In the fashionable stereotype of the time, Irishmen were lazy; thus a dozen of them would not get much work done.

6. Mauling rails means to hit them very hard with a maul, a wooden hammer used for driving stakes, wedges, and the like.

7. The term *Jack's house* usually refers to a slap-dash hotel or boarding house although Byrn is referring here to a state penitentiary. A *jack-house* is a slang term for a privy, and Byrn is possibly making a pun here.

8. Meaning that it considerably dampened his bravery. This is the first known appearance in print of the phrase; for a list of other nineteenth-century works in which it appeared see Taylor and Whiting, p. 372.

9. See note 4, chapter 1.

10. Probably another instance of Byrn playing around with a proverbial saying. The phrase "to bring a hornet's nest around one" is old and well established, but the line used by Byrn is otherwise unreported.

11. Another example of the way Byrn changed some traditional sayings around. The usual phrase is "as quiet as a cat."

12. Another example of a traditional sounding phrase that is probably an invention of Byrn's.

13. Sheep generally travel in the company of the rest of their flock, especially at night. Thus, a lone animal in a forest at night would likely be very scared.

14. Probably another change by Byrn of the usual phrase, which is "puffing like a steam engine."

15. The term *chicken-hearted* was relatively common in folk tradition but only rarely found in published writings of the nineteenth and early twentieth century. For examples of its use, see Brunvand, p. 24.

16. Fears involving touching the dead are numerous, but there are also contradictory beliefs. The idea that touching the dead is to be avoided is contradicted by the belief that touching a dead person may be beneficial. Touching of the corpse may symbolize some sort of settling of accounts, or it may merely free one from the fear of a dead person. Relevant here also is the belief that it is bad luck to take anything away from a cemetery. See Wayland D. Hand, Anna Casetta, and Sondra B. Thiederman, *Popular Beliefs and Superstitions: A Compendium of American Folklore From the Ohio Collection of Newbell Niles Puckett* (Boston: G. K. Hall and Company, 1981), p. 1245.

17. Another traditional sounding phrase that probably was coined by Byrn.

18. Also probably a saying coined by Byrn.

19. I have been unable to identify either of the men mentioned here or *blithersdorf*, which seems to be a German nonsense word.

20. Byrn probably means here a ridiculous effort, although he could be referring to some folktales in which a man disappears by rubbing his nose with a cow's horn or by rubbing the horn.

21. Again, a phrase probably coined by Byrn.

22. The phrase "like a duck on a June bug" is otherwise unreported, although "like a dog on a June bug" is traditional.

Chapter V

1. Obviously a phony name made up by Byrn and probably modeled on the stage oratory of the minstrel show, a form of entertainment that was very popular in 1851.

2. Another proverbial saying that was either coined by Byrn or has remained otherwise unreported.

3. A believer in ghosts would be classed among the most superstitious persons, especially by someone in the 1850s who considered himself a scientist.

4. A reference to one of the hunting exploits of David Crockett (1786–1836) recounted in *A Narrative of the Life of David Crockett of the State of Tennessee* (1834; reprint, Knoxville: The University of Tennessee Press, 1973), pp. 162–164. Crockett wounded the bear, who then tried to get away from him by climbing a large black oak tree. Eventually Crockett was successful in killing the beast. In the first half of the nineteenth century Crockett was very popular, primarily because of the almanacs published under his name in the 1830s. These volumes are generally considered the first examples of Southwestern humor.

5. *Haunted* is used here in the sense of nervous, annoyed, or pestered, rather than in the sense of feeling visited by a spectre.

6. A candlestick without wick or tallow would, of course, be good for nothing but show.

7. The rooster, of course, rules the roost in a hen house, so Byrn means here that the dog walked in as though he were in charge of the office.

8. Hollering.

9. The first published appearance of the proverbial phrase "like a hot potato" was in Richard Henry Dana, Jr.'s, *Two Years Before the Mast, A Personal Narrative* (1840). For other appearances of the phrase in literary works, see Taylor and Whiting, p. 294; Brunvand, p. 112.

10. Probably another invention of Byrn's rather than a proverbial saying.

11. The term *negro revenge* refers to an especially cowardly way of getting revenge. The very existence of the term is an indication of the regard in which blacks were held at the time.

12. Some people believe that the term *barn dance,* referring to a country dance, was originally called a *bran dance* because the floors were usually covered with bran. This etymology, however, is mostly assumption and awaits definitive proof.

13. In other words, extremely small pieces. This is another saying that probably was coined by Byrn.

14. Spunk is a dry, partially decayed piece of wood. In Byrn's day and earlier, people used spunk to catch the sparks from the flint-and-steel gadgets they carried in place of matches.

15. In other words, he couldn't be a friend. There is a widely known tall tale relevant to the incident Byrn relates concerning a hog that accidentally eats some dynamite and then gets kicked by a mule causing an explosion that does vast damage and leaves the animal sick for several days. Byrn's story, of course, has the animal meeting a more tragic end. It is very similar to the following item reportedly told by Abraham Lincoln:

Well, Bill Sykes had a long, *yaller* dog, that was forever getting into the neighbors' meat-houses and chicken-coops. They had tried to kill it a hundred times, but the dog was always too smart for them. Finally, one of them got a bladder of a coon, and filled it up with powder, tying the neck around a piece of punk. When he saw the dog coming he fired the punk, split open a hot biscuit and put the bladder in, then buttered all nicely and threw it out. The dog swallowed it at a gulp. Pretty soon there was an explosion. The head of the dog lit on the porch, the fore-legs caught astraddle the fence, the hind-legs fell in the ditch, and the rest of the dog lay around loose. Pretty soon Bill Sykes came along, and the neighbor said: 'Bill, I guess there ain't much of that dog of your'n left.' 'Well, no,' said Bill; 'I see plenty of pieces, but I guess that dog, *as a dog,* ain't of much more account.' (Paul M. Zall, *Abe Lincoln Laughing: Humorous Anecdotes from Original Sources by and about Abraham Lincoln* [Berkeley: University of California Press, 1982], p. 115)

Lincoln used the anecdote in comparing Confederate General J. B. Hood's army, which was defeated in December, 1864, to Bill Sykes's dog. According to Zall's notes, Lincoln also told it about Slocum and his dog, Bill. Francis F. Browne, in *The Every-Day Life of Abraham Lincoln* (New York: N. D. Thompson, 1887), pp. 616–617, says Lincoln told the anecdote on another occasion but the deed of "blowing up" the yellow dog was done by "mischievous small boys."

16. The stereotypical Irishman has an almost limitless appetite for alcoholic beverages.

17. See note 4, chapter 4.

18. The first appearance in print of the proverbial term "walking papers" was in Henry C. Lewis's, *Odd Leaves from the Life of a Louisiana "Swamp Doctor"* (1843). Lewis wrote under the pseudonym of Madison Tensas and is generally thought to have influenced Byrn's writings, particularly the *Life and Adventures of an Arkansaw Doctor.* See Masterson, *Tall Tales of Arkansaw,* pp. 88, 335. For more examples of the use of the phrase in literary works see Taylor and Whiting, p. 393; Brunvand, p. 150.

19. Probably another saying coined by Byrn.

20. The very popular proverbial phrase "get your dander up" appeared in a number of nineteenth-century writings, of which the first was *A Narrative of the Life of David Crockett of the State of Tennessee* (1834). For other appearances of the phrase, see Taylor and Whiting, p. 90; Brunvand, p. 32.

21. "As ever you saw a man in all creation" is a very popular proverbial phrase meaning as can be observed anywhere.

22. That is, to go get it sharpened.

23. The proverbial phrase "mean as a Jew" and "bad as a Jew" are common in folk tradition and in literary sources, but "mad as a Jew" appears in no proverb dictionaries I have been able to consult. For examples of the other related phrases, see Frances M. Barbour, *Proverbs and Proverbial Phrases of Illinois* (Carbondale and Edwardsville: Southern Illinois University Press, 1965), pp. 99–100; Taylor and Whiting, p. 204.

24. This may be a parody of a song, but, if so, it is a long forgotten one.

25. Rackensack is a derisive name for Arkansas, here referring to a person from Arkansas.

Chapter VI

1. This is, apparently, a parody on the title "I'll Hang My Harp On a Willow Tree," a song said to be of ancient English origin but in some nineteenth century songbooks attributed to a W. Guernsey. This was Wellington Guernsey who is listed as the lyricist-composer on a sheet music edition published in Louisville, Kentucky, in 1848 or 1849 by W. C. Peters & Co. At least two possibilities exist concerning Guernsey's connection with the song. First, it is possible that he was merely an arranger and had nothing to do with the creation of the song. The fact that he is given total credit on the sheet music does not preclude this possibility. A second probability is that Guernsey wrote the lyrics and set them to an older tune; this would explain the frequent references to the song as an ancient English number. However, approximately two years before the Guernsey edition appeared, a sheet music edition, arranged for voice and guitar, was published in Philadelphia. This edition of c. 1846 was arranged by Leopold Meignen and made no mention of Guernsey.

2. This is obviously a take-off on the name of Shakespeare, a favorite person for parodies on the minstrel show stage.

3. That is, as though she had no strength to do otherwise.

4. Slipping off.

5. The original says "bands of matrimony," but this is probably a typographical error.

6. See note 5, chapter 2.

7. A dido is a rowdy prank or an overly exuberant caper. The expression "to cut a dido" is well established in folk tradition and also was utilized in a number of nineteenth century publications, of which the first was Joseph C. Neal, *Charcoal Sketches* (1837). For a list of other publications in which the phrase appeared, see Taylor and Whiting, pp. 101–102.

Chapter VII

1. In the nineteenth century *consumption* was the most frequently used name for tuberculosis.

Chapter VIII

1. Toting.

2. Possibly a reference to a cannon.

3. The word *easy* is used here to mean quiet or quietly.

4. The proverbial phrase "give one the bag to hold" means to leave a person in the lurch or to engage their attention in order to deceive. The earliest known appearance of the phrase is contained in G. D. Scull, ed., *Journals of John Montresor* (New York: New York Historical Society, 1881), which dates from 1760 but were not published until 1881. The phrase was also used by, among others, Thomas Jefferson. For various published examples of the phrase, see Whiting, p. 19; Taylor and Whiting, p. 14; Farmer and Henley, 1:97.

5. It is possible that this is a misprint and that Byrn really meant to use the word *wagged,* meaning to carry an object or person about. I have been unable to find any printed reference using *waged* in this sense.

6. *Baby-wakers* refers, of course, to the explosive. The reference to Amos Jackson is previously unreported.

7. *Sprout* in slang usually refers to a bunch of twigs, but that is not necessarily the meaning implied here. The reference here is probably to some sort of flower that blooms in the spring; thus when it is cut much moisture comes from it, i.e., it bleeds.

8. The proverbial phrase "as ugly as a mud fence" is widely known in folk tradition. For examples, see Archer Taylor, *Proverbial Comparisons and Similes from California* (Berkeley: University of California Press, 1954), pp. 48–49; *The Frank C. Brown Collection of North Carolina Folklore,* 1:448. The longer form of this phrase is "as ugly as a mud fence in a thunder storm."

9. The usual phrase is "like a dog in high (or tall) rye"; thus Byrn either has changed the wording slightly or merely repeats a traditional saying that has been otherwise unreported.

10. The usual saying is "like a hog on ice" or "as independent as a hog on ice." This is another instance where Byrn either changed the wording slightly or is repeating a traditional saying that has otherwise gone unreported.

11. The name *Koot* is, in all likelihood, not an actual name but

merely a means for Byrn to make further fun of these people and, at the same time, avoid a possible lawsuit. *Coot* is a slang term, primarily used in America, referring to a stupid or silly person.

Chapter IX

1. Most medical authorities from the time of Hippocrates until approximately 1860 believed in drawing blood for the relief of pain. The bleeding was usually performed by cutting people with a sharp knife. In some cases, blood letting was achieved by means of leeches, a practice still followed in some very traditional circles. Healthy persons engaged in the practice on a regular basis in order to purify the blood. In the Middle Ages and in colonial America barbers often served dual duty as surgeons and thus performed the bleedings. The barber pole is said to be reminiscent of that era; the white band represents the bandages used by the surgeons (i.e., barbers), and the red stripes indicate the blood.

Yet, even though bleeding was almost universally practiced from ancient times, not everyone agreed with the method. Ambrose Pare (1510–1590), sometimes called the father of modern surgery, was the first man of his century to protest the practice of indiscriminate bleeding. Guy Patin, a prominent medical teacher of the seventeenth century, characterized the surgeons of his day as "a race of evil, extravagant coxcombs, who wore mustaches and flourished razors." But the most common attitude of the time was expressed by a poetically inclined phlebotomist:

> Of bleeding many profits grow, and great,
> The spirits and the senses are renewed thereby,
> Tho these men slowly by the strength of mate
> But these by wine restored are bye and bye:
> By bleeding to the marrow cometh health.
> It maketh clene your brane, releeves your eie,
> It mendeth appetite, restoreth sleepe,
> Correcting humors, that do waking keepe
> All inward parts, and senses also clearing.
> It mends the voice, the smell, the hearing.

See Donald T. Atkinson, *Magic, Myth and Medicine* (Cleveland: The World Publishing Company, 1956), pp. 148–149.

2. Holler.

3. A joke dependent upon the surprise ending and relatively typical of the sort of jokes used in minstrel shows, although I am unable to cite any exact parallels. In minstrel shows the joke would most likely have been given in the form of a conundrum. For some examples, see anonymous, *Minstrel Gags and End Men's Handbook* (1875; reprint, Upper Saddle River, New Jersey: Literature House, 1969), pp. 28–29.

4. Byrn's tendency to pun seems unlimited. Here he toys with the term *scrape,* meaning a fight or some sort of trouble, and *scrapings,* meaning the lowest possible thing in, for this instance, the entire world.

5. Syndesmology is the anatomy of the ligaments, hence anyone working on them is practicing syndesmology.

6. *Venesection,* also known as phlebotomy, refers to the practice of opening a vein for letting blood as a therapeutic measure.

7. A narrow valley or cove. In folk speech the word is often pronounced "holler."

8. *Ramstuginous* is a word apparently made up by Byrn, who was following a stereotype of the time. Frontier people, minority groups, and anyone else held to be an inferior were often given to using language in unintelligible or grandiose ways, at least on stage. It was also the way persons who imagined themselves intellectuals were depicted on stage and in much popular literature. The best known example is the minstrel show where blacks and the interlocutor, who was usually white, were both known for their use of high sounding but ultimately meaningless words.

9. Another apparently invented proverbial phrase.

10. *Frolic* was the word generally used in the country to describe a dance with instrumental accompaniment, usually consisting of a fiddle and sometimes a banjo.

11. "Hain't" is a very popular dialect contraction of "have not."

12. In other words, to see all of the fun.

13. In other words, he would hit her very hard. A dog chasing a polecat or skunk would be very determined until he got sprayed.

14. This is Byrn's version of the standard fight scene found in most

examples of Southwestern humor. It generally consisted of much eye-gouging, ear biting, and the like.

15. That is, in its original place.

Chapter X

1. A popular song of 1843 by A. F. Winnemore and Charles T. White was entitled "Stop Dat Knocking at De Door" and may well be the song referred to in this parody.

2. Dr. Byrn wrote some thirty books, mostly on medical and religious topics, and contributed three further books of humor. These include *Rattlehead's Travels: or, The Recollections of a Backwoodsman, That Has Travelled Many Thousand Miles on the Highway of Human Destiny; Brought About a Revolution in Domestic Happiness; and Affected a General Shake-up of Creation* (1852), the *Rattlehead's Chronicles* cited in chapter 3, note 7, and *The Rambles of Fudge Fumble, or the Love Scrapes of a Life Time* (1860). This seems to be adequate proof that *Life and Adventures of an Arkansaw Doctor* did meet with some public favor. Added to this is Byrn's own, probably inflated, statement that *Life and Adventures* and its sequels sold in the millions. There seems little doubt, though, that they sold very well, otherwise the subsequent volumes would not have been published. See Masterson, "The Arkansaw Doctor", p. 42.

3. At the time Byrn was writing many doctors prescribed calomel (mercurous chloride), a white tasteless powder that acted as a laxative, no matter what the problem. So common was this situation that Judson J. Hutchinson (1817–1859), of the famous Hutchinson Family Singers, lampooned the practice in the song "Go Call the Doctor, and Be Quick or Anti-Calomel," which was something of a hit in the 1840s.

4. Cupping glasses were used in bleeding a patient. Blood was drawn to the surface of the skin by means of the vacuum created by the glass.

5. That is, they were moving fast like a boat at full sail.

6. The proverbial phrase "to cut a shine," meaning "to make a show" or "make an impression," has long been popular with American writers. Its first published appearance was in *The Poems of Philip Freneau*

(1787). For other appearances of the phrase in literary works, see Whiting, p. 389; Taylor and Whiting, p. 326; Brunvand, p. 125.

7. *Glutei* is the plural form of *gluteus* and refers to any of the three muscles that form each of the buttocks and act to extend, abduct, and rotate the thigh.

8. Aqua fortis is nitric acid.

9. Byrn is quite right in stating that this is an old saying, although it is usually worded "kill or cure." The oldest known reference to it is in 1684, but it is also found in John Wise, *The Churches Quarrel Espoused* (1713), and in Governeur Morris's *Diary* maintained during the French Revolution. For other reports of the phrase, see Whiting, p. 244.

10. *Sensorium* refers to the whole sensory apparatus of the body, so *sensorium commune* means, in this instance, that the young man's entire sensory apparatus was affected.

Chapter XI

1. A widow. This still common usage is quite ancient, appearing in, among other places, the King James version of the New Testament. There are, of course, many other redundant combinations that are very traditional and still in common use. For a list and discussion of some of these, see Vance Randolph and George P. Wilson, *Down In the Holler: A Gallery of Ozark Folk Speech* (Norman: University of Oklahoma Press, 1953), pp. 52–54.

2. The usual phrase is "grin and bear it," in which form it has been collected traditionally in California, New York, and Illinois, although it is probably more widely known than this collecting record indicates. The earliest known reference to the phrase is in 1774, but it was very popular in nineteenth-century literature. For various appearances of the phrase see Whiting, p. 188; Taylor and Whiting, p. 162; and Barbour, p. 81.

3. *Diggins* or *diggings* refers to one's place of residence or employment. *Dry* refers to a lack of something or to a place where something either does not occur or is forbidden, as in the case of legal liquor. Thus, the term *dry diggins* used here simply means that they did not have parties where they were from, or at least did not call them that.

4. The proverbial phrase "know which end is up" is well known in several forms including "know which end he stands on," "know which end his head was on," and "know which end of the stick is up." For various nineteenth-century publications in which this phrase appears, see Taylor and Whiting, pp. 120–121.

5. Although the phrase "mad as a wet hen" is of long-standing folk tradition in the United States, it has only rarely been noted in print. The first known appearance of the phrase in a published work is in Joseph Doddridge's *The Dialogue of the Backwoodsman and the Dandy* (1821). For other publications in which it appears, see Whiting, p. 210; Taylor and Whiting, p. 181. The item is well established in folk tradition and has been reported from Illinois, Texas, New York, Indiana, Arkansas, New Hampshire, Tennessee, Connecticut, Nebraska, Alabama, and California. See Barbour, p. 89; Taylor, *Proverbial Comparisons and Similes From California*, p. 56.

6. *Hoosier*, of course, refers to a person from Indiana, but it also is a derogatory term referring to a tramp, dirty person, or someone who is in most ways inferior. The Hoosier of stereotype was described by Davy Crockett in one of his almanacs:

> Now the Hoosiers are a different class o' human natur altogether. They are half taller an' bristles, an' so all-sweaten fat and round, that when they go to bed they roll about like a cider barrel in a cellar, an' therefore they're always obleeged to have a nigger each side on 'em to keep 'em still; an' when they wake up, they have to fasten down their cheeks before they can open their eyes. A Hoosier can eat a hog, tail, fur and all, and in the fall of the year, the bristles come out on him so splendifferous thick that he has a regular nateral tippet about his throat, an' a nateral hogskin cap on his head. I once had one of these half starved critters to work on my plantation—till one hot day come, an' if he didn't spill his hull self, nails, hair and all, into my hay wagon, then cut me up for shoe greasers; an' arter we cooled it, thar he was a complete cake o' hog fat, an thar' was enough on him to grease all the harnesses and wagons for a hull year. (From Richard M. Dorson, *Davy Crockett: American Comic Legend* [1939; reprint, New York: Arno Press, 1977], pp. 123–124.)

Thus, what Byrn means is that the person was somewhat crude. In *Tall Tales of Arkansaw,* Masterson quotes a passage from Father Dennis Alphonsus Quinn's "A Synopsis of Missionary Life in Eastern Arkansas" in his *Heroes and Heroines of Memphis* (1887), which proclaims that "the country Arkansian, when designated from his city brother, is always called 'the *Hoosier.*'" (Masterson, p. 8). Later, Masterson notes that "this application of *Hoosier* in Arkansas seems to have been noted only by Father Quinn" (Masterson, p. 308). Perhaps Byrn, writing thirty-six years earlier, was the first to note this particular usage.

7. Camphene is a colorless, crystalline compound, prepared synthetically from pinene and used like camphor, i.e., as an irritant and stimulant.

8. Meaning he was dejected. This phrase is both quite popular and quite old, first being noted in print in 1608. It also appears in one of the plays of William Congreve, the English dramatist, and in numerous published American writings. See Whiting, p. 301; Taylor and Whiting, p. 253; Farmer and Henley, 4:367. It has also been collected from oral tradition by Frank C. Brown, 1:567.

9. Meaning that he thought he was very good at dancing. The proverbial phrase has a long history in the United States, being noted among the sayings used in early New England in Richard M. Dorson, *Jonathan Draws the Long Bow* (Cambridge: Harvard University Press, 1946), p. 51. For various published usages, see Taylor and Whiting, p. 298; Farmer and Henley, 5:322. The phrase has also frequently been reported from folk tradition and has been collected in Illinois, Texas, New York, Indiana, Connecticut, Nebraska, Alabama, and Oregon. According to a note in Maximilian Schele de Vere, *Americanisms: The English of the New World* (1871; reprint, New York: Johnson Reprint Corporation, 1968), p. 237, "Bostonians are said to have derived, from their attachment to this vegetable, and the esteem in which it is universally held among them, the phrase *Some Pumpkins* expressive of high appreciation," but he goes on to note "that this explanation of the term is not the true one, although the latter cannot well be stated, because it would offend ears polite."

10. The proverbial phrase "flat as a pancake" is quite widespread in folk tradition, having been collected in California, New York, Tennessee, Texas, Washington, Nebraska, and North Carolina, and is probably even more widely known than this list indicates. For references to collections from oral tradition, see Barbour, pp. 71, 134. It was

also quite popular with nineteenth-century writers, being found in, among other places, Thomas C. Halliburton's *The Clockmaker; or The Sayings and Doings of Samuel Slick of Slickville* (1838). The earliest known reference is in a 1774 entry in Janet Schaw's *Journal,* E. W. and C. M. Andrews, eds. (New Haven, 1934). For various literary uses of the phrase, see Whiting, p. 326; Taylor and Whiting, p. 275.

   11. That is, indefinitely adjourned.

Chapter XII

   1. *Row* is a slang word for disturbance or trouble. The first printed evidence of the word is in a magazine published in 1794, although it may well predate that publication. In any event, it was well established prior to 1851 when Byrn was writing. For more information on the term see Farmer and Henley, 6:63.

   2. A joke is intended here. Rather than say "I will go to hell," Byrn says he will go to Arkansas, a state which in the nineteenth century had, in some quarters, the reputation of being not much better than hell. Of course, many traditional anecdotes about unusually hot weather were told about Arkansas. For example, see Vance Randolph, *We Always Lie to Strangers: Tall Tales From the Ozarks* (New York: Columbia University Press, 1951), pp. 183–185.

   3. His stay in this "land of strangers" was relatively brief, lasting at most only two years. By 1853 he was living in New York City, where he maintained medical offices until his death in 1903.

   4. The usual phrase is "don't know enough to come in out of the rain" or "too dumb to come in out of the rain" or "so dumb that he won't (or can't) come in out of the rain." Widely known in folk tradition, this saying has been collected in Texas, Illinois, Indiana, Nebraska, Tennessee, North Carolina, Ohio, and Washington and is probably more widely known than that list indicates.

   5. Ague is a fever, usually caused by malaria, marked by regularly recurring chills.

   6. Byrn's daughter, Mrs. Charles J. Stevenson of Baldwin, Long Island, told James R. Masterson that her father claimed the Hanly letter

was real and that he would gladly show it to anyone, essentially the same claim he makes in this book. Despite his willingness, Mrs. Stevenson never actually saw the letter. See Masterson, "The Arkansaw Doctor," p. 49.

7. *Bottom* as used here refers to a valley, a common usage in the South.

8. The proverbial phrase "gone sucker" saw frequent usage in nineteenth-century literature. It first appeared in Thomas C. Halliburton, *The Attache; or Sam Slick in England* (1843); and John S. Robb, *Streaks of Squatter Life* (1843). For a list of other appearances of the phrase, see Taylor and Whiting, p. 359; Brunvand, p. 137.

9. There are a number of folk beliefs that involve observing the actions of horses to predict oncoming weather. It is said that if horses refuse to drink in very dry weather then it is a sign that a cloudburst will be happening shortly. When horses suddenly stop feeding and start scratching themselves on trees or fences, then heavy rains are going to come shortly. If horses run and kick up their heels and whinny in the fields, it is a good indicator that an electrical storm is at hand. Another related belief is that when horses sweat, sniff loudly, and switch their tails violently, then rain is arriving shortly. For these, and similar beliefs, see Vance Randolph, *Ozark Magic and Folklore* (New York: Dover Publications, Inc., 1964; originally published as *Ozark Superstitions,* New York: Columbia University Press, 1947), pp. 10–33; Puckett, p. 1490; and Brown, 7:308. The exact form given by Byrn is not found in any source I have examined, but there is no good reason to believe that he made it up; it sounds very traditional.

10. That is, the summer. A pun here.

11. A similar line is told in Thomas W. Jackson's *On a Slow Train Through Arkansaw,* ed. W. K. McNeil (Lexington: The University Press of Kentucky, 1985), p. 43.

12. Panthers were once common in the South, particularly in the highland areas, but are now almost unknown. The panther is, of course, a mountain lion.

Chapter XIII

1. Doctor Thompson's identity is unknown, assuming, of course, that the reference is to an actual person.

2. The phrase is usually "as plain as the nose on your face," so Byrn once again has made a slight change in the traditional saying. The expression cropped up frequently in eighteenth- and nineteenth-century writings. For lists of these, see Whiting, pp. 313–314; Taylor and Whiting, p. 263; Brunvand, p. 100. It has been collected from oral tradition in Illinois, California, Texas, Tennessee, and Nebraska. See Barbour, p. 130.

3. The exact phrase used by Byrn has not been reported in any dictionary of proverbs that I have been able to examine, although several very similar usages are found. These included "don't tear your shirt," "if I ain't as much mistaken as the man who lost his shirt," "you are as much mistaken as if you had burnt your shirt," and "won't last longer than a paper shirt in a bear fight." This seems evidence enough that Byrn did not invent the phrase wholecloth.

4. That is, his stomach.

5. Another of Byrn's puns, this one revolving on the word *job*, meaning a piece of work, and *job* or *jab*, meaning to prod or thrust suddenly against.

6. A trocar, or trochar, is a surgical instrument consisting of a sharp stylet, i.e., a slender probe used for examining wounds, enclosed in a tube (cannula) and inserted through the containing wall of a body cavity. The stylet is withdrawn, permitting fluid to drain off through the tube.

7. See note 6.

8. Another pun. *Dropsy* is a name for edema, which is a disease characterized by an abnormal accumulation of fluid in cells, tissues, and cavities of the body resulting in swelling. Thus, when the stylet was withdrawn an excessive amount of fluid should have come out.

9. The phrase "the jig is up" was quite popular in late eighteenth- and nineteenth-century writings. For a list of the publications in which it appears, see Whiting, pp. 239–240; Taylor and Whiting, p. 204; Brunvand, p. 78; Farmer and Henley, 4:54.

10. A preparation from the dried roots of the ipecac plant, a South American creeping plant with small, drooping flowers. The preparation is traditionally used in the treatment of laryngitis, bronchitis, and chronic diarrhea.

11. That is, like a horse that had no control over himself, moving around as if he were drunk.

Chapter XIV

1. "Sugar in the Gourd" is the name of an instrumental tune, popular on the nineteenth-century minstrel stage, which was reprinted in a number of tune collections. Although many Southern fiddlers use the same title, they generally apply it to a variant of "Turkey in the Straw," also a nineteenth-century minstrel show tune. The lyrics used for both tunes includes a statement "Sugar in the gourd, The way to get it out" which is then followed by instructions on how to get it out; these are thinly disguised sexual references.

2. *Red lane* is a slang term for the throat and is quite ancient, being noted as early as 1566. See Farmer and Henley, 6:8.

3. There is no exact parallel to this phrase in any proverb dictionary I have examined, although a traditional saying "Bad (or eager) as a pig after slop" is reported from Illinois. See Barbour, p. 139. Thus, it seems that here is another example of a saying that was rearranged by Byrn.

4. Snarly, or tangled, oak.

5. That is, britches made out of the coarse or broken part of flax or hemp, which is called *tow.*

6. "Go to Jericho" is a slang term meaning "go to the devil."

7. There are many traditional narratives about haunted places that people are afraid to visit, although usually the fear doesn't really keep persons away from the sites. A popular motif in stories of ghost lore and spirit hauntings is the man who will be given a house or property if he can stay overnight in a haunted place. This motif, found in both Europe and the United States, is listed in Thompson's index as H1411 "Fear test: staying in haunted house" and H1410 "Fear test: staying in frightful place."

8. A widely traveled folk belief is that a horse can see a ghost and will balk. This has been reported from folk tradition in North Carolina, Maryland, Kentucky, Alabama, New York, Ohio, Illinois, and is probably known in other places where it has not been collected, Arkansas, for example.

9. The proverbial phrase "as white as snow" is still popular, although it has been in use for well over three centuries. Its first known usage in this country is in 1629 when it was used by Thomas Hutchinson in an entry in his papers. Bartlett Jere Whiting, the noted proverb scholar, counted sixty-one occurrences of the phrase in the next two centuries. See Whiting, p. 403. In addition, Whiting and Archer Taylor discovered at least seventeen more usages in the popular literature of the period 1820–1880. See Taylor and Whiting, p. 342. Jan H. Brunvand also located six usages in books published by Indiana authors 1816–1890. See Brunvand, p. 130. It has also been reported from folk tradition in Illinois, California, Tennessee, North Carolina, and Nebraska and is probably much more widely known in oral tradition than this last list indicates.

10. Meaning enormous or great.

11. *Gubbing* probably means throwing it up. The word *gub* means lump, but I have been unable to locate the word *gubbing* in any slang dictionary.

Chapter XV

1. Asafetida (or asafoetida or assafoetida) is a bad-smelling gum resin obtained from various plants of the carrot family that is used in medicine as an anti-spasmodic. In folk medicine asafoetida bags were used to ward off colds and other similar ailments.

2. Tolerable. This usage is at least as old as Shakespeare, who used it in at least one of his plays, *All's Well That Ends Well* (1603).

3. This is, of course, a version of the Arkansas Traveler dialogue; indeed, it is the earliest known printed example, although, in this instance, there is a boy rather than a squatter. For an extended discussion of this dialogue, see Masterson, *Tall Tales of Arkansaw*, pp. 186–219. Of

course, similar dialogues were quite popular in American theater of the time.

4. The proverbial phrase "to make my (or one's) hair stand on end" was very popular with nineteenth-century writers, first appearing in William Cobbett's *Porcupine's Works* (London, 1801). See Whiting, p. 192; Taylor and Whiting, p. 167; Brunvand, p. 64.

5. During the era in which Byrn was writing, he would have had ample opportunity to read about Indians and their captives, for, beginning in the sixteenth century and continuing throughout most of the nineteenth century, captivity narratives were relatively commonplace. Almost without exception these publications were not sympathetic towards the Indian, although their propaganda was also not always just anti-Indian: sometimes they were anti-French or anti-British, depending on when they were produced. Even some persons who should have known better were influenced by the propaganda of these captivity narratives. Thus, George Bancroft (1800–1891) in his *History of the United States* (1834–1874) uses episodes found in captivity narratives to convey his negative beliefs regarding the place of the Indian in American society. The captivity narratives also colored the work of Francis Parkman (1823–1893), particularly his *The Conspiracy of Pontiac* (1851). Many American novelists, including Charles Brockden Brown, James Fenimore Cooper, William Gilmore Simms, and Herman Melville, also used the patterns of the Indian captivity narratives in their work. For more about this phenomenon, see James Levernier and Hennig Cohen, *The Indians and Their Captives* (Westport, Connecticut: Greenwood Press, 1977).

6. It is unclear what tribe Byrn was captured by.

7. Probably another proverbial phrase made up by Byrn. At least, it does not appear in any proverb dictionary.

8. Although there are many folk remedies for stopping blood and even some people who claim to have special powers to do so, the method employed by the Indians in Byrn's book is the most elementary.

9. That is, they were asleep. See note 6, chapter 1.

ChapterXVI

1. That is, a ferocious beating.

2. There is a body of folk belief, common not only to the United States but to Europe as well, that holds that animals of various types can live in a person's stomach. Usually they get into the human body through drinking water or by the person swallowing the animal's semen or egg, although here the accident supposedly occurred while the man was sleeping on a woodpile. Relevant motifs here are B784 "Animal lives in person's stomach"; B784.1 "How animal gets into person's stomach (or body) (various methods)"; and B784.2.4 "Physician removes animal from stomach of patient." For a recent article discussing another instance of a person who supposedly had a snake living in their body, see Donald J. Sawyer, "The Lady With the Snake in Her," *New York Folklore Quarterly* 25 (December 1969): 299–305.

3. This phrase as used here may represent nothing more than Byrn falling back on stereotypical stage talk for blacks, but it is traditional in some parts of Arkansas to use the adjective *heap* in combination with a noun such as *money*. See Randolph and Wilson, p. 251.

4. This is a reference to pokeberry juice, which is derived from the reddish-purple berry of the pokeweed and is traditionally used for treatment of a variety of ailments.

5. "To cut a caper" means to do something prankish and has been popular in this country for well over two hundred years. Its first known appearance here was in a paper written by Benjamin Franklin in 1737. For other citations, see Whiting, pp. 56–57; Taylor and Whiting, p. 56. For references to the phrase collected from oral tradition, see Barbour, p. 29.

6. *Lobelia inflata,* better known as Indian tobacco, which is used as an emetic or expectorant.

7. The proverbial phrase "dead as a mackerel" did not often appear in nineteenth-century American writing. Indeed, its first known printing is in the present book. For a list of other publications in which it appears see Taylor and Whiting, p. 232. The saying is frequently encountered in American folk tradition, being reported from Illinois, Tennessee, Texas, and Washington.

8. That is, extremely large gnats.

9. This is an example of Byrn's use of hyperbole. There are some traditional Arkansas tall tales about huge bull frogs, some of which are associated with Pine Bluff, which is situated on the Arkansas River. See Randolph, *We Always Lie To Strangers,* pp. 70–71.

10. Although there are many proverbial comparisons involving lightning, the one given by Byrn has rarely been reported from folk tradition. The comparison usually involves *greased, oiled, chain,* or *red lightning* but rarely *blue lightning.* It seems to have been rarely used, if at all, by other nineteenth-century American writers.

11. *Sassenger* is a slang term, generally considered rather vulgar, for sausage. The word is also spelled *sassiger.*

Chapter XVII

1. A popular song of 1843 was Michael William Balfe and Alfred Bunn's "I Dreamt I Dwelt In Marble Halls," one of the selections in their opera *Bohemian Girl;* it is possibly the song being parodied here. Balfe (1806–1870), an Irish singer and composer, had a number of popular song hits in mid-nineteenth-century America of which none were more successful than the already mentioned song and two others, "The Heart Bowed Down" and "Then You'll Remember Me," from *Bohemian Girl.*

2. The proverbial phrase "dead as a hammer" has not often been used in American writing. Its earliest known such appearance is in the anonymous poem "Yankee Phrases", *Port Folio* 3 (1803): 87. It is also found in John T. Irving's *The Attorney: or, The Correspondence of John Quod* (New York: 1842). It has been collected from oral tradition in Illinois, North Carolina, and Texas.

3. I have not been able to identify the exact name of the *bull vine leaf.*

4. A *simblin* or *simbling* or *simlin* is a species of summer squash, which obviously makes no sense in the present context. Byrn was apparently using a local, otherwise unrecorded slang term or simply making up a word.

5. A reference to the medical act of drawing blood to the surface of the skin by means of the vacuum created in a cupping glass. There is both dry cupping, which is achieved without cutting the skin, and wet cupping, achieved by the application of a cupping glass to a cut surface. For more about the practice of bleeding, see note 1, chapter 9.

6. The usual saying is "quicker than (or as quick as) you can say Jack Robinson." The Commodore Perry referred to here is Oliver Hazard Perry (1785–1819), the American naval officer who defeated the British at the Battle of Lake Erie during the War of 1812. In 1854, shortly after Byrn's book was published, Perry's brother, Matthew Galbraith Perry (1794–1858), gained fame for negotiating the first treaty between Japan and the United States.

7. That is, in difficulties or disfavor.

8. A diluent is anything that dilutes or dissolves, but in medicine the term is used to refer to any substance that thins the blood.

Chapter XVIII

1. *Ager* is a colloquial way of saying *ague*, a word referring to a fever, probably caused by malaria, that produces regularly recurring chills. *Bone-rattle ager* means that the chills were extremely severe.

2. Brandy toddy is a drink made of brandy mixed with hot water, sugar, and, usually, spices. In folk medicine it is often used to treat colds.

3. A sugar house is, of course, a place where sugar is processed; especially a building where maple sap is boiled to produce maple syrup or sugar. Because of the heat necessary to boil the sap, there would be quite a bit of sweating or moisture. This seems to be another "proverbial" phrase coined by Byrn; at least it does not appear in any proverb dictionary.

4. Threshing machine.

Chapter XIX

1. Slaves were valued according to their physical condition. Thus, a slave who was deaf would have been considered defective and of less monetary value on the slave market.

2. That is, he was faking his "defect." The expression refers to the habit of the opossum, which throws itself on its back and feigns death on the approach of an enemy. Apparently, the term first became popular with writers in the nineteenth century; no usages of it prior to Timothy Flint's *Geography of the Mississippi Valley* (1828) have yet been found. See Farmer and Henley, 5:261.

Chapter XX

1. A misspelling of *carotid,* the two great arteries of the neck. These are the two principal arteries that convey blood from the aorta to the head; one is located on each side of the neck.